FASHION HACKS

THIS IS A CARLTON BOOK

This edition first published in 2016 by Carlton Books
An imprint of the Carlton Books Group
20 Mortimer Street
London W1T 3JW

First edition published in 2008

A CIP catalogue record for this book is available from the British Library.

ISBN 978 1 78097 704 1

Printed and bound in China

Illustrations: Sam Loman

FASHION HACKS

500
STYLISH WARDROBE SOLUTIONS
FROM HEAD TO TOE

Caroline Jones and Fiona Wright

CARLTON
BOOKS

CONTENTS

INTRODUCTION

Did you know that slingback shoes flatter everyone or that the right underwear can take off 10 lbs (4.5 kg), or even that a wide belt can help give you a waist if you have a boyish figure?

From tips for creating a capsule wardrobe and dressing for your particular body shape to finding the right shoe for your outfit or the best date dress, this book contains 500 fashion hacks to show you how small changes in what you wear can make a huge difference to your appearance. Advice on solving fashion disasters and fashion secrets from top stylists are also included to help you look polished, groomed and gorgeous from head to toe – whether you go.

TOP TEN FASHION HACKS

BAG A GREAT WAISTLINE
(see Handbags, page 12)

WINTER WEAR
(see Coats & jackets, page 31)

HALTER EGO
(see Beachwear, page 41)

IT'S A WRAP
(see Special occasion dressing, page 65)

ACCENTUATE THE LESS OBVIOUS
(see Date clothes, page 73)

STREAMLINE YOUR SUITCASE
(see Travel fashion, page 83)

AVOID SWEAT MARKS
(see Gym and sportswear, page 92)

FIND THE REAL THING
(see Vintage & second-hand clothes, page 108)

ANTI-STATIC
(see Stylists' secrets, page 111)

INSIDE OUT
(see Care & cleaning of clothes, page 119)

ACCESSORIES

SHOES

BEWARE ANKLE BOOTS
Boots that stop just above the ankle can be difficult to wear with dresses or skirts as they cut off the leg at the slenderest point. Unless you are very thin and the shoe is very form-fitting, your best bet is to go for the lower-cut shoe boot.

NO-NOS FOR MINIS
Never team heavy shoes with minis; especially avoid Oxford shoes, clogs or bulky shoes, which will make your feet look huge in comparison. Although padded cross-trainers (sneakers) are a definite no-no, trainers can be cute when worn with minis or denim skirts. Choose plimsolls like Keds for a preppy look or Converses for a sceney urban style.

TREAT YOUR FEET
You don't have to suffer to look great in heels – buy shoes that are slightly roomier so you can add gel inserts for extra comfort under the balls of your feet. Most pharmacies sell them and they fit neatly into your handbag for sore-feet emergencies.

BOOT IT IN
Forget spiky heels in winter and inclement weather and instead choose shoe boots. Low-cut shoe boots are a less bulky choice than other boots for wearing under trousers or skinny jeans and look modern when worn with short skirts or dresses.

PLATFORM POWER

High-rise platforms are a strong look and can add height without discomfort. Slim-heeled versions look good with suits or evening dresses while chunkier styles are fun and adventurous. The most comfortable types are those where the sole actually bends when you walk – where the platform is restricted to the areas at the ball of the foot and the heel.

MATCH LIGHTNESS

Strappy sandals are the favourite choice for formal eveningwear where even open-toed or peep shoes will look too heavy. If the look is light – your dress is floaty or exposing – your shoes should reflect it. Bronze, silver or gold sandals are good choices, but make sure you match the metallic colour to your jewellery and any hardware on your bags.

HEEL KNOW-HOW

The thicker the heel tip, the more comfortable and stable the shoes will feel. Small heels, especially stilettos, will wear down more quickly.

SUMMERTIME SHOES

Kitten heels and slingbacks are great choices for summer wear when you don't want to show your toes or the weather's a bit chilly or rainy. They look good with either trousers or skirts.

TRY THE TOE TEST

With closed toes, make sure you can still wiggle your toes. If you can't do this, the shoes are too tight and may cut off your circulation – leading to numb toes by the end of the night. Tight shoes can also lead to ingrown toenails and bunions.

MAKE MINE A MARY JANE

Originally an Edwardian shoe with a round toe, strap and buckle, and a popular choice for the 'little girl' look, Mary Janes are now most often seen as stack-heel styles. The updated MJ, such as the two-tone type by Marc Jacobs, is much more versatile than the traditional styles as it has very high heels and looks good with skirts or trousers.

THE VERSATILE WEDGE

More comfortable than stilettos, wedge sandals are a fantastic summer choice for wearing with dresses, jeans, gauchos or even shorts if you've got the legs. Wedges can also be found on boot and pump styles in materials ranging from casual suedes and textured materials to fine leathers and metallics.

HOT FEET

Always try on shoes towards the end of a shopping trip when your feet are at their hottest and most swollen to get a better idea of how they will fit.

PUT COMFORT FIRST

High heels push your weight forward onto the balls of your feet so check to see how cushioned this area is before you hand over your credit card.

PICK THE PERFECT HEEL

Even if you're a little on the short side, don't be tempted to go for killer heels all the time – they can make you totter and look as though you're trying too hard. Instead, try wearing medium-sized or kitten heels, which provide the ideal combination of height to give you confidence and elegance to elongate your legs.

PUMP UP THE VOLUME

Flat shoes such as ballet pumps look lovely when worn with short skirts and minis, but never wear them with longer skirts. Flat shoes can appear to add weight to the leg but this is counterbalanced by exposing more area of the leg.

DOUBLE DUTY

Similarly check if any of your shoes need new soles or heels and drop them off at your local shoe bar. To save time, choose an outlet that does dry-cleaning as well – so you can have both chores done at once.

SHOE SHAPERS

Ideally, keep all your shoes in shoe trees when not in use. This will extend their life, maintain their shape, prevent creases and keep them dry. Renowned for its aroma and drying properties, cedarwood is the best material for shoe trees as it's ideal for keeping footwear fresh and dry. Cedar will absorb foot moisture, acids and salts and reduce cracking and deterioration.

HANDBAGS

KEEP IT CLASSIC

If you are lucky enough to afford a designer bag, it's much more of an investment to go for a style that will stand the test of time rather than the latest 'it' bag. Look for classic shapes and colours such as black or tan.

BAG A GREAT WAISTLINE

If you have a tiny waist, choose a bag that hangs just above it: this will draw the eye to that particular area and helps accentuate it.

TLC FOR BAGS

To keep expensive handbags looking their best, store them in drawstring cotton bags when not in use and keep them in the top of your wardrobe – rather than at the bottom with shoes – to prevent them from being squashed out of shape.

MATCH YOUR LOOK

Make sure the style of your bag suits the outfit you are wearing. When you are going for a girly look, don't choose a black studded leather bag; similarly, a bright red patent bag is great for 'rock chick' style but floral cotton won't work at all.

PICK A HOBO

A good everyday choice is the hobo handbag. Roomy and slouchy, it has a short shoulder strap to allow a snug fit under the arm, making it hard for purse-snatchers to grab and keeping contents safe and secure.

MATCH THE SEASONS

Think carefully about which fabrics are right for which season. Velvet and dark leather bags are great for winter; while in summer try bags made from wicker, cotton and brightly coloured leather.

WEAR AND CARE

Keep leather and suede bags in top condition by treating them with waterproof sprays once a month, and where possible avoid using them in rainy weather.

REMEMBER PROPORTION

When choosing a new bag, always try it on in front of a mirror as the style may not suit the proportions of your body. Oversized bags can look ridiculous on very tiny or short women and they can also hide or block you and your clothing from view. Likewise, tiny bags on big women can look silly. Think about the overall look the bag creates on your body.

FIRST IMPRESSIONS COUNT

For interviews and meetings, make sure your bag is functional and smart. Choose one that can easily hold a CV (résumé) or business proposal, as well as having pockets to keep business cards, pens and your phone easily accessible – so you're not scrabbling around for them.

BAGS OF FUN

When you want to make a statement, look for bags with unusual detailing such as feathers, studs, fake fur and embroidery. If the colours are neutral, they will go with any outfit but still catch the eye and make an impact.

CLASSY CLUTCHES

A clutch bag, usually worn in the evening, creates an elegant look. Often called pochettes, the small, envelope-style, understated versions of the clutch are quietly chic, though you may want to try one of the fashionable oversized clutches that grab attention.

JUNK IT

Make sure you set aside time to regularly de-clutter your handbag. Fact: some of us carry up to 3.5 kg (7 lb) of personal items in our bags and in the long term this can damage posture and trigger back and shoulder pain.

VINTAGE FINDS

Check out vintage fairs for one-off styles. Slightly battered leather bags can look fantastic with jeans or slung across a pretty floral summer dress.

JOIN THE CHAIN GANG

Look for evening bags with detachable chains or chains that can be tucked neatly inside – then, depending on your outfit, you can wear them on your shoulder or as a clutch bag.

HOT METAL

A metallic gold or bronze bag looks good in the summer, worn against a white summer dress and a tan.

CLUTCH CONTROL

Swapping your normal day bag for a cute clutch is an easy way to dress up your work outfit for a night out. Choose snakeskin or sequined styles for a touch of glamour.

LIFE'S A BEACH

Summer holiday bags should have a relaxed look – but as they will more than likely end up being stained with suntan lotion and grass marks, don't invest a huge amount. Buy cheap bags that are brightly coloured and can hold your book and a beach outfit plus your towel.

CARRY A TOTE FOR SHOPPING

Totes and shoppers are great styles for shopping as they have one main compartment for stashing the items that you have bought. Hung from the shoulder, they usually fall at about elbow length. Often made of canvas and open at the top, totes are very large and sturdy. They are also ideal for outdoor activities such as sailing or going to the beach.

GO HANDS-FREE

If you are a hands-on person who hates the hassle or restrictiveness of carrying a bag, choose a style with a strap that can be worn across the body.

BAG FOR LIFE

Keep a reusable cloth bag neatly folded inside your handbag at all times. Then, whenever you buy anything, you'll avoid damaging the environment any further as you won't need a plastic bag.

ON-THE-GO BAGS

Satchels, also known as messenger bags, are ideal for students and travellers as they have long straps so they can be worn across the body, thus leaving the hands free. They are characterized by outer pockets for storing items to which you need easy and quick access.

JEWELLERY

WRIST ACTION
The wrists are a very sensual part of the body so don't forget to draw attention to yours. If you have slender wrists, a delicate chain or slim bangle will look great, while chunkier shapes suit larger wrists.

JEWELLERY SWAP SHOP
At some stage most of us are given pieces we don't like, only to have them sit at the bottom of our jewellery box. But one person's trash is another's treasure so get together with friends and swap pieces – you're bound to find something each of you prefers.

GET THE LENGTH RIGHT
Tops with deep or scooped necklines offer a great frame for shorter necklaces while v-necks suit longer pendant necklaces. If your big bust makes you self-conscious, avoid wearing a necklace that nestles into your cleavage and draws attention to it.

ROCK ON
Thanks to costume jewellery, it's now perfectly possible to wear a big rock on your finger for a fraction of the cost. Keep a selection of rings with different coloured stones and metals to match different outfits.

HALT STOP!
When wearing halter-neck tops the neck is already a focal point because of the fabric tied around it, so there's no need to add a necklace – it can even look odd. Instead, draw attention to your bare shoulders with a pair of drop or hooped earrings.

QUANTITY, NOT QUALITY

For a laid-back appearance that's totally up to date, try layering necklaces of different lengths. This works best with thin gold chains – the longer the better.

GO DANGLE

Just putting your hair up and wearing a pair of glitzy earrings completely changes the tone of an outfit. Hoops and vintage beads will go with most clothes and provide an interesting focal point for otherwise ordinary looks.

GO FOR CHOKE

A striking choker necklace worn with a strapless top or dress breaks up an outfit and adds extra glamour to the bare skin on show. Look for a beaded style of necklace that picks up on one or more of the colours in your outfit, or add sparkle to a black dress with Audrey Hepburn-style diamanté.

PIN IT TOGETHER

A well-placed brooch livens up a little black dress and adds a splash of instant colour to your coat or sweater. Keep an eye out for vintage cameos or jewelled brooches in interesting shapes in second-hand stores and antique markets.

LAYER BANGLES

Adding a few bangles instantly livens up an outfit and there are hundreds of different styles out there to choose from. Look for bangles made of wood or bright Perspex – it's all about being bold and stacking them up.

SCARVES, WRAPS & BELTS

FAKE IT

For a classy 1950s evening look, try a fake-fur stole. Go for simple black, white or cream with a ribbon attached that you can throw around your shoulders and tie in a bow at your chest or neck.

ORGANIZE YOUR ACCESSORIES

If you have the wardrobe space, invest in a scarf hanger, which has holes for the scarves to pull through. Your scarves will never be creased again and the hanger can be used for everything from silk scarves to pashminas. A belt hanger is also a good idea so that you can easily see and choose the item you want for your outfit. Make sure you buy one that enables you to take off items and replace them one by one rather than a hoop style.

BELT IT

Belts are an instant way to add glamour to a plain outfit or dress, so look for styles that have interesting or intricate detailing. Belts can also provide a more affordable way of wearing designer items – and another advantage is that they will last for years.

OTHER ACCESSORIES

USE YOUR HEAD

Not everyone suits the same shape of hat so choose carefully. Knitted berets look good with hair tucked up inside or with short styles, while 'beanies' suit wearers with long sleek hair. Wide brims are good for larger heads and neat pillar-box styles are perfect for smaller heads.

ADD A HAT

Nothing attracts attention quite like a hat. It takes confidence
to wear one so choose classic shapes such as a fedora or beret to
make the look easier to pull off.

PICK THE RIGHT SHADES

Perhaps the most versatile item you can own is a great pair of
sunglasses. They add an air of mystery and can look stylish
when worn on top of your head. Keep a few pairs of sunglasses
including oversized and vintage so that you have something to
suit every occasion.

ADDING A PERSONAL TOUCH

BREATHE NEW LIFE INTO OLD OUTFITS

Cash-flow crisis? Before you buy a new outfit for a special occasion, see if an existing favourite can be dressed up with funky accessories. A cool hat or striking choker may be all that is needed.

STOCK UP ON SNIPPETS

Your accessory drawer is your box of tricks when it comes to updating your look or transforming an otherwise dull outfit. Keep it stocked with plenty of inexpensive belts, scarves and jewellery, adding a few new pieces each season so that you always look up-to-the-minute.

PLAY UP THE POSITIVES

Use accessories to draw attention to a part of your body that you like, such as a pair of sapphire earrings to accentuate your blue eyes or a cinched-in belt to show off your tiny waist.

A BIT OF BLING

Use statement accessories to bring a plain outfit to life. For example, team intricate diamanté earrings or belts with streamlined, simple black dresses or jeans.

KEEP IT SIMPLE

Never over-accessorize. Wearing killer heels, a big necklace and a flashy belt at the same time can make an outfit confusing. For maximum impact, stick with just one or two key items at a time.

WARDROBE BASICS

COLOUR CODING

THE COLOUR TEST

Different colours suit different women – it depends on whether your skin has a cool or warm undertone. To find out, hold a piece of plain white paper under your hand and look closely at the colour of your skin. If the overall hue of your hand is blue-ish, you have a cool skin tone, while if you see yellow, you have a warm skin tone.

WARM UNDERTONE

If you have a warm skin undertone, the best colours to flatter your complexion are earthy tones – browns, beige, olive, peach, corals and gold or yellows.

COOL UNDERTONE

If you have a cool skin undertone – which means a pink or rosy tone, you will look best in colours from the blue, green and purple family – shades such as pale blue, rose pink and purple.

GOLD OR SILVER?

If you have a warm complexion, silver can look stunning, while gold will warm up cooler skin tones. To find out which one works for you, hold a piece of gold fabric up next to your face and then swap it for silver and see which colour makes your face look brighter.

SUMMER TIME

Women who have 'summer' colouring will have grey-blue eyes mixed in with some hazel or green colourings and their hair is often dark blonde or brunette. They look great in denim and neutral colours such as cream, tan and navy. For a splash of colour, summer types should wear pastel colours such as pale mint, dusky raspberry and pinks.

WINTER WONDERS

Women with dark brown to black hair, dark brown or green eyes, and olive skin are likely to fall into the 'winter' category. For neutral clothes, look for items in black, charcoal grey and dark navy; for colour, winters look great in regal purples, emerald green, magenta and burgundy.

AUTUMN BEAUTY

If you are an 'autumn' woman, you will match the colour of the season with bronze, copper or ginger hair and warm, golden skin undertones. You may have very pale skin with freckles. Flame red, gold, deep teal, dark orange and olive colours work best for autumns. For neutral shades, try khaki, coffee and cream tones.

STEP INTO SPRING

Women with 'spring' colouring are recognizable for a peaches-and-cream complexion that tans easily. Their eyes tend to be light and their hair colour is often wheat, strawberry blonde or brown. The best shades to wear are those that mirror the season, such as peach, apricot and sunny yellows, light blue, plus bright aqua and turquoise.

ORIENTAL STYLE

Women with oriental skin have a slightly peachy tone to their colouring and look great in white clothes. Pale colours also work well but women of this skin type can achieve an instant sophisticated look by wearing black.

CAPSULE COLLECTION

STAY NEUTRAL

A capsule wardrobe full of neutral shades can reduce the amount of time you have to spend putting looks together because you already have basics that work together. Keep to black, navy, grey, beige, cream and white.

CHOOSE ANY COLOUR ...

So long as it's black! Black is a fail-safe colour that never goes out of fashion. Staple blacks should form the basis of any capsule wardrobe, so make sure you have a good strong collection of classic trousers, jackets, skirts, dresses and tops in different weights of fabric.

ACCESSORIZE YOUR CLASSICS

Each item in your capsule wardrobe should be a classic fit that can be worn year after year and accessorized or lifted with on-trend items. Choose cheaper items such as blouses and fashionable skirts to add each season, which will introduce pattern and colour.

CAPSULE ACCESSORIES

THE RIGHT BOX OF TRICKS

A capsule wardrobe should exude groomed put-together style, so don't ruin it by throwing on any old piece of jewellery. Make sure accessories complement not just your outfit but each other, too. One long and one short simple necklace are must-haves.

STYLISH SUNGLASSES

For real glamour, pick up a stylish pair of sunglasses. Take a friend with you when looking for the right pair and try on as many shapes and styles as you can so that you find the perfect sunglasses for your face shape.

THE ULTIMATE LEATHER HANDBAG

A well-made classic leather bag will last you for years and instantly adds style and sophistication to your look. Perfect for work, interviews and meetings, it's worth investing a bit more in a great bag – and with leather you get what you pay for.

SMART WITH A SCARF

A square silk scarf is indispensable (Grace Kelly used her Hermès scarf as a sling for a broken arm!). It can jazz up any outfit, from a little black dress to a business suit or jeans and a jacket. It can be worn as a belt, halter-top, sarong, as a shawl over a jacket, on the head, or to accent a handbag. Or tie it round the neck!

STICK THE BOOT IN

Finding the right boot to flatter your leg and suit your style can take time – but persevere. A smart pair of knee-high boots should be an important part of your winter wardrobe as they look great with skirts and dresses and suit almost all legs shapes, as they hide chunky calves and ankles.

BASIC KNITWEAR ESSENTIALS

CLASSY CASHMERE

Although expensive, a cashmere sweater will hold its shape, feel amazing and never go out of style. It is super-soft, lightweight and offers 'breathability'. The highest class of natural fibre (from Kashmir goats), cashmere can be worn with smart trousers or jeans and works well in both summer and winter. The number of times you will end up wearing the sweater means that its cost per wear makes it a worthwhile investment.

FANTASTIC FABRIC

Go for a fine-wool knit jumper (sweater) and keep the shape tailored but simple. Merino is durable, soft and resistant to creasing and wear. Don't be tempted to go for the latest fur trim or funnel neck shape – it will look dated by next year. Stick to a classic design and you can wear it year after year with different scarves and gloves.

BASIC SHIRTS & TOPS

SHOP FOR TOPS

Fitted T-shirts and vests in a wide variety of colours are the staples of any versatile wardrobe. For a great shape, choose fabrics with a hint of stretch – but not too much or they will cling to lumps and bumps. A ribbed white-and-black vest top goes with everything and can be worn alone or under other tops and dresses.

SOFTLY SOFTLY

A floaty chiffon blouse that can be teamed with capsule skirts or trousers can add femininity to a sharp-tailored look and break up a hard silhouette. Choose ones that are lined to avoid the see-through problem.

THE CLASSIC WHITE SHIRT

A tailored shirt will look great for work and can also be dressed down with jeans at the weekend. Choose good-quality cotton for crispness.

DRESSING FOR YOUR SHAPE

SKIRTS & DRESSES

SUMMER LOVING

A pretty summer dress is a must-have. Choose one that can be worn for both day and evening summer events. Floral is timeless, while block colours can date.

DRESS TO IMPRESS

An easy day-to-evening dress is simple to pull off and requires no thinking – you can concentrate on the accessories you'll wear with it rather than worry if the top works with the skirt or trousers. Look for something with classic lines that will show off your best features, whether that's your legs, bust or waistline.

DAY AND NIGHT

A dark knee-length skirt is an essential. Skinny girls should choose A-line shapes while pencil skirts suit those with curvier figures. A simple skirt like this can be worn with a plain fitted top or shirt for daytime and then vamped up with a sexy, shimmery top for the evening.

DRESS ME DOWN

Smart enough for work but laidback enough for weekends and holidays, a great shirtdress is always an investment buy. For maximum versatility, keep it fitted and in a subtle colour.

COATS & JACKETS

WINTER WEAR

A good winter coat is one of the most important items you will buy, so spend time getting the right one. Remember, you will be wearing it most days so it needs to be versatile – a mid-length works for most needs. Avoid boxy styles, which can look frumpy, and choose one with a shaped waist that will suit all figures. A dark wool or cashmere blend will last year after year.

THE SCRUNCH TEST

Always check the crumple potential of any coat. Grab a handful of fabric and squeeze it hard for ten seconds. If it looks crumpled, so will you.

CHECK THE FIT

The mark of a coat that fits well is that you can cross your arms in front of you and still reach up comfortably. Make sure the coat tapers in at the waist, fits snugly on the shoulders and that the sleeves aren't below the middle of your thumb in length.

GET INTO A TRENCH

A well-fitting trench coat is smart enough to wear to work, but also perfect when teamed with jeans for a stylish weekend look. Go for a light-coloured one as a contrast to your dark winter coat.

TROUSERS & SUITS

LOOSE-FIT TROUSERS

Loose-fit trousers, à la Kate Hepburn, should be worn with a tight shirt to balance out the volume. Loose worn with loose looks sloppy, and tight on tight can look trashy. Tailored classic neutral-coloured trousers with a turn-up (cuff) look especially smart.

DREAM DENIM

Jeans are a key staple. A well-cut pair can be dressed up or down depending on the occasion. It's a good idea to have at least two pairs of well-fitting jeans – one pair in a darker shade for winter and a second pair in a lighter colour for summer.

LOVELY LINEN

A flattering pair of linen trousers is key to your wardrobe. By choosing a pair in a neutral shade you'll look perfect during those tricky transitional months between summer and winter. Choose beige rather than white as the trousers will stay looking smarter for longer and show less dirt.

SUITED SEPARATES

For a great-fitting suit, choose a label that offers separates so you can choose a different fit for the jacket and trousers. Many women are a different size top and bottom and it is rare that an off-the-peg suit will fit perfectly.

SUIT IT UP

A well-cut trouser suit is one of the best items you can buy for your capsule wardrobe. The trousers should be straight-out or bootleg, with flat fronts (no pleats) and enough stretch for comfort. Pockets on the jacket or trousers should be without flaps to keep the look streamlined.

FINDING THE PERFECT JEANS

JEAN-IUS!

Often people don't realize that a good tailor can alter jeans to give a perfect fit. Jeans that fit in the leg but are too big in the waist can be taken in while panels may be added to the sides of jeans for extra room. If they're too long in the leg, it's well worth paying to have your jeans taken up. Not only will they look better, they'll also last longer as you won't be constantly treading on the hems.

THE HIPS DON'T LIE

Fact: Many women are pear-shaped – especially in the West – and hipster jeans are the most flattering for this figure. They'll make your bottom look small, your waist tiny and, if worn with heels, they'll give you long and elegant legs.

LOVE YOUR LYCRA

If you're apple-shaped, go for jeans with a bit of added stretch as this will help slim your tummy area. Slim-fits will flatter your small bottom while low-waisters disguise a thick waistline.

HOW TO WEAR YOUR JEANS

Jeans can be worn with heels, tucked into boots, with ballet pumps or with trainers. When shopping for jeans, consider which type of footwear you plan to wear with your jeans as it will influence the length and the shape. Skinny jeans look great tucked into boots, for example, but boy-fit slouchy ones don't.

BUY IN PAIRS

Finding the perfect pair of jeans is no easy feat so when you discover the right style for you, buy two pairs. When one falls into disrepair, you won't be devastated if you find they've been discontinued.

SKINNY WITH STYLE

Though skinny jeans refuse to go away, they can be hard to pull off. Wear them with a good pair of heels; flat ballet pumps are a popular choice but they make even the slinkiest celebrities seem larger-hipped.

EARNING THEIR KEEP

Jeans are probably the hardest-working item in your wardrobe so it's worth spending a bit of time to work out what style best suits your figure before you part with your hard-earned cash. Visit your nearest department store or jeans specialist to try on the 10–15 pairs you like to discover what does – and doesn't – suit you.

LONG TALL SALLY

If you're tall, you can get away with pretty much any shape or style of jeans. Show off your long pins with low-rise, straight-legged styles and roll up the bottoms in summer for a casual look. Look out for extra-long versions of standard jeans now made by most manufacturers.

DON'T LET THEM FADE AWAY

The best way to keep dark indigo colours vivid is to wash them in cold water with only a little detergent and to dry them indoors rather than on a line outside where they can be faded by the sun. Iron your jeans inside out to avoid leaving any shiny scorch marks.

JEANS TLC

Most denim specialists advise leaving jeans well alone. Washing them too often causes fading and wear and tear, so only wash them when it's really necessary. Denim is a hardwearing fabric that doesn't get dirty or start to smell easily. If you can't bear to leave your jeans, make sure that when you do wash them you choose a cool cycle and they are turned inside out.

THE DARKER, THE BETTER

Unless you're ultra-thin, stay away from very light-coloured or stonewashed jeans. Dark jeans make everyone look slimmer and will go with just about anything.

THE LONGER, THE BETTER

When you go shopping, wear a pair of shoes with heels similar to those you usually wear with jeans. Keep in mind that when jeans shrink, so too can the length, which means it's better to go for the longer pair.

LOVELY LINGERIE

AVOID BACK PROBLEMS

A poorly fitted bra can not only be unsightly under clothes but also can be unhealthy. If the bust is not well supported, the breasts will fall to the bottom of the cup and put extra strain on the shoulders and neck to support the weight of the breasts. An underwired bra provides extra support underneath the bust.

CHECK THE SIZE

To make sure your bra fits correctly, your finger should be able to pass underneath the band at the front, and the middle of the bra should lie flat against your breastbone. If the back of the bra rides up, you probably need a smaller size; if your breasts squeeze over the top of the cups, but all else feels fine, then you need a bigger cup size. The straps should not dig in or fall off the shoulder – make sure you have adjustable straps so that you can alter the fit.

CALL IN THE PROFESSIONALS

Always wear a professionally fitted bra. Have your bust measured at your local department store or underwear shop to ensure a perfect fit. A recent survey found that 60% of women were wearing the wrong size bra.

BALCONY BRAS FOR SMALLER BREASTS

A balcony bra can give you an enhanced neckline, excellent
uplift, and a lovely, curvy shape. Half-cup bras also flatter
a smaller bust; padding at the sides and under the bust give
maximum lift. Avoid bras that have square-cut bust lines; they'll
flatten you even more.

AVOID THE PINCH

Take a good look at the bras you wear every day and consider
whether they truly fit you as well as they could. A good bra gives you
a continuous smooth line and should not create any bulges under the
arms, across the back, under the breast or across the cleavage.

BIG BOSOMS

Large-breasted women should always get a professional fit;
a good bra will lift the breasts and define the waist, plus
provide support for heavy breasts. A thick band rather than an
underwire often provides better support. A minimizer bra can be
a good choice under suits.

BE A SMOOTHIE

Invest in some smooth, well-shaped underwear that fits
perfectly. Good panties should hold in any lumps and help
improve your posture. Power panties like Spanx create a smooth
line and are super slimming – they also carry further down the
leg to tighten the whole area while still feeling sexy.

KNOW YOUR CUP SIZE

Measure your chest just under the breasts. If the number is
even, add 4 inches; if the number is odd, add 5 inches. Now
measure the fullest width across your breasts. If the numbers
are the same you are an A cup; if 1 inch more, a B; if 2 inches
more, a C; if 3 inches more, a D; if 4 inches more a DD.

MATCH YOUR BRA TO YOUR CLOTHES

Different bras provide different functions. For a streamlined
look under tailored office clothes, wear a bra with a bit of uplift
and firmer support. For casual wear, you may prefer a softer
seamless bra to go under clingy tops and T-shirts. If your weight
varies due to hormone fluctuations throughout the month,
choose a bra with some Lycra, which will adjust more readily to
the changes.

REAR VIEW MIRROR

Always check out your back view in a full-length mirror before you go out, watching out for VPL or other unsightly bumps and bulges. Remember that your rear view is 50% of what people see – which is a big percentage!

FLESH IT OUT

White underwear will show through sheer summer clothes. Unless this is intentional (and if you're not Madonna, it shouldn't be), choose the correct colour bra and pants. The key is to wear undies in flesh tones that match the colour of your skin, not the outfit. If in doubt, they should be one shade darker than your skin. Try to shop wearing neutral underwear so you can see exactly how a sheer item will look.

BEACHWEAR

TALL AND SHORT OF IT

If you're tall, to avoid looking like a beanpole on the beach, don't go for up-and-down stripes, high necklines or solid block colours. Tall women can carry off brightly coloured swimwear, and bikini shorts are perfect for slim hips. If you prefer wearing all-in-ones to bikinis, look out for waist detail or belts on bikini bottoms to give your body more waist definition.

HAVE AT LEAST FOUR

Make sure you have a collection of swimsuits for all situations and for numerous changes, especially if you take more than one beach holiday a year. Have at least four: two that provide more coverage and can be worn for swimming lengths and two for tanning.

HIP-SWINGING

Pear shapes should wear a darker bottom and a brighter top
to draw attention away from their bigger bottom half. High-cut
bikini bottoms make your butt look smaller and your legs longer.

LITTLE UP TOP

If you are small on top, look for bikini tops that have built-in
padding or underwiring. Details such as ruffles or prints will
create the illusion of curves.

INVEST IN THE BEST

You never show off your body more than on the beach or by the
pool, so do it justice by buying a really well-fitting, flattering
swimsuit. All-in-one pieces and bikinis alike should give firm,
uplifting support and hold you in, in all the right places. For
the top, make sure you consider all the factors you would when
buying a bra.

HALTER EGO

For those with bigger busts, halter-neck top bikinis not only
offer support but create enviable cleavage, too. Go for tops that
provide some support and have thicker straps – they will be
more comfortable. And look for one-piece swimsuits with built-in
structure such as soft foam cups.

PATTERN PRINCIPLES

Patterns on swimsuits can have the effect of making the eye
concentrate on the pattern instead of what lurks behind it!
Choose the pattern depending on your shape. The smaller you
are, the smaller the pattern you can get away with, but on a fuller
figure a small and delicate pattern will enhance your size, so go
for a larger and bolder pattern that your body can carry off.

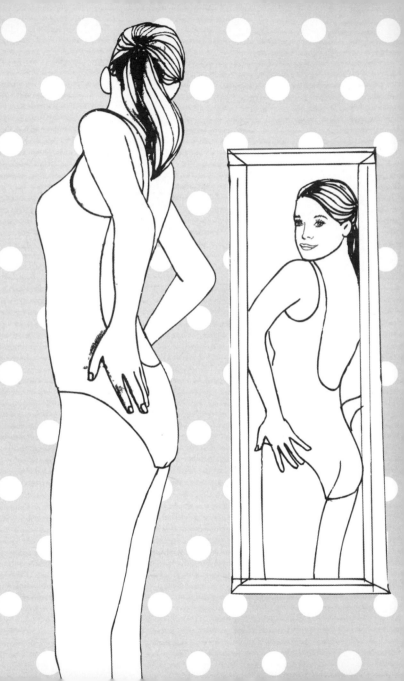

CHOOSE A BIKINI FOR YOUR BODY

There are almost as many styles of bikinis as figures to fit them. Look at your body type and decide what you want to accent and what you want to detract from. For example, bra-tops are best for those who are big on top, while leggy girls might want to hide their middle with a tankini. Take time to get the right size – too small and too big are equally disastrous.

CHOOSING A ONE-PIECE

When selecting a one-piece, make sure it is long enough to stay in place when you walk, otherwise it will ride up. Stand, sit, bend and walk in it before you buy to ensure that the suit is comfortable is snug enough to cup your bottom without cutting in. If it bulges or cuts, try a bigger size; if it droops, try a smaller one.

BELLY FLOP

If you don't like your tummy, try a tankini or look for an all-in-one that has a lower back to draw attention to a more flattering area.

TRY IT ON

When shopping for swimwear, try on as many different styles as you can, as those you might have dismissed in the past – such as strings, halter-necks or boy short styles – may actually suit your figure. Even a 1940s high-waisted style might give you an old-school glamour that suits your personality.

ORGANIZING YOUR WARDROBE

MIND YOUR GAP

Watch out for gaps in your wardrobe.

For example, you might have plenty of great tops, but a serious shortage of skirts and trousers to wear them with. Shop cleverly to make all the clothes in your wardrobe work hard.

PUT CLOTHES IN ORDER OF COLOUR

Arrange your clothes by colour – for example, red, orange, yellow, green, blue, and so on, interspersing white and black between the brightest shades. It makes your wardrobe look pretty and gives you fresh ideas on what clothes to mix and match.

ONLY KEEP WHAT FLATTERs

Hold on to what suits you. Don't keep 15 pairs of OK-fitting trousers – throw out all but the most flattering. Make sure you have different lengths of trousers to wear with heels and with flats, plus if you have short legs, have any over-long trousers taken up so they look as if they were made just for you.

WINTER STORAGE

Put freshly laundered winter sweaters in paper bags (not plastic) for storage during the summer months. T-shirts, scarves and jeans can all be stored in this way in the winter, too.

LINE YOUR DRAWERS

Protect your clothing from wood acid, which can cause fabric to deteriorate, by lining your clothes drawers with acid-free paper or quilted fabric. Never use wallpaper remnants – the sweet-smelling backing can attract insects to your clothing.

HAVE A CLEAR-OUT

Streamline your unruly clothes collection into a
flexible, stylish wardrobe that works for you by
having a giant clear-out. Throw everything onto the
bed and take a long, critical look at what's there.
Be ruthless when throwing things out – every
item has to earn its keep.

PACK THEM IN

Never hang up silk or woollen sweaters. Always fold and place them on shelves using layers of tissue paper where possible.

CHALK IT UP

Keep your nicely decluttered wardrobe damp-free by hanging up chalk tied on a length of string. The chalk sticks help to reduce moisture in the air and keep your wardrobe smelling fresher.

GO WIRELESS

Buy some good-quality wooden or padded hangers and throw away freebie wire ones that can damage the shape of your clothes.

GROUP AND ROTATE

Group together all your trousers, skirts, dresses and jackets so you know exactly where to find things. If something moves to the back, bring it to the front. You will find this means you wear all your clothes an equal amount instead of always choosing the same old thing.

STORE IT WELL

Keep evening and wedding dresses in large, nylon garment bags designed for the job. Alternatively, store them in boxes with acid-free tissue (which insects do not like) to keep them in good condition.

SUCK IT IN

Vacuum packing is a cheap and safe way to store clothes, and it's also space-saving. Buy special bags fitted with a round rubber hole that allows an ordinary vacuum cleaner nozzle to be inserted to suck out all the air.

BEAT THE MOTHS

Moths love nothing more than cashmere and silk, so avoid giving them an expensive meal by ensuring your clothes are clean when you put them away (sweat and food stains attract moths) and invest in some cedarwood mothballs.

LOOKING SLIMMER

DARK HORSE

Although scientists aren't sure why this is, it's a fact that a tan gives the illusion of a slimmer figure. But stick to fake tans rather than baking in the sun or using sunbeds – both of which can cause premature ageing and skin cancer.

THE RIGHT SIZE

There's no point in getting a size smaller simply because you hate having to buy the size you really are. In fact, a smaller size will be tighter and actually make you look bigger. If it really bothers you, cut the labels out (most are inaccurate anyway!) but buy clothes that fit and flatter.

WALK TALL

Stand with your shoulders back, your back straight and your head held high. This simple trick will elongate your body and make you appear at least a size thinner.

DOWN, NOT ACROSS

Horizontal lines can make you look wider, while verticals and pinstripes are much more flattering and make you seem much taller.

CHOOSE CLOTH CAREFULLY

Avoid stiff and heavy fabrics or anything too clingy such as thin jersey or Lycra that will show off all the bits you want to hide. Opt instead for lightweight fabrics such as cashmere or fine-weave cotton that skim your curves rather than stick to them.

SKIRT AROUND IT

If you're not confident about your legs, choose the length of your skirt carefully. Skirts that fall just above the knee can make legs look stumpy. Mid-thigh or just-below-the-knee lengths are much better bets as they emphasize slim calves.

GRACEFULLY GREY

While it's true that wearing dark colours makes you look slimmer, you don't always have to restrict yourself to black. Navy, charcoal or dark grey all have the same flattering effect and are less harsh on paler skin tones.

MAKE PATTERNS WORK FOR YOU

Small patterns can make larger shapes look smaller, while the smaller you are, the larger the pattern you can carry off.

HORSING AROUND

It may sound simple but pulling your hair up into a high ponytail gives the appearance of an instantly thinner face and a longer neck.

FLAUNT IT!

Instead of concentrating on the parts of your body that you want to hide, focus and flaunt your positive points – sexy ankles, pretty toes, great lips, silky shoulders – everyone has something.

CUT-OFF POINT

The longer the length of your trousers, the thinner they will make your legs look. Teaming long trousers with a pair of heels doubles the result. Cut-offs, pedal-pushers and shorts, on the other hand, all steal length from your legs.

JACKETS OFF

When wearing a jacket, make sure you're happy to take it off. If your jacket is covering a multitude of sins, such as a top that makes you look (or feel) fat or jeans that create bottom bulge, you'll feel compelled to keep it on. Wear a slimming, fitted cotton top underneath and carry a scarf to drape over yourself if it makes you feel more confident when you take your jacket off.

BOYISH FIGURES

YOU'VE A BOYISH FIGURE IF ...

Your bust and hips are a similar width, your bust is fairly small and you have no defined waist. Your bottom is probably neat and flat and you have long slim legs. Make the most of your body shape by using the following tips ...

IT'S A CINCH

Athletic or boyish-shaped women lack a defined waist but you can create one with a wide eye-catching belt. Cinch it over a loose blouse and full skirt for maximum effect.

FAKE IT

For a special occasion or a night out, fake your shape. Use structured clothing such as a sexy basque or a laced corset top with hipster jeans.

DEAD CERT

Shirts can look too masculine on boyish figures but a cleverly cut white shirt with a small ruffle at the neck and a waist tie will soften your look and add a waist while still being smart enough for work.

SHOW SOME LEG

Because you have naturally long legs, you are lucky enough to suit most hemline lengths, so make the most of your legs by wearing a mini. Make it an A-line shape, not tight, so the skirt gives you more of a waist.

PERFECTLY WRAPPED

Look out for wrap dresses in clingy soft jersey that have weight and hang well. The diagonal line of the dress creates the illusion of shape. Add a belt for extra definition to give you a waist and curvier hips.

BULK OUT

Belted coats with pockets on the hips add bulk and emphasize your hips and waist. A mac with padded shoulders also provides width on top, making your waist seem narrower. Make sure the belt is a different colour to add the impression of extra curves.

EASY, TIGER!

While most women are advised to steer clear of horizontal stripes, boyish figures can easily get away with them because of your slim upper-body shape. They will also help to create the illusion of a bigger bust.

TROUSER TRICKS

If your legs are long and thin, then skinny jeans and straight satin cigarette trousers can look great on you. Make sure you wear a different shape on top, such as a loose-fitting cotton top cinched in at the waist or an empire-line blouse, to avoid the 'beanpole' look.

GIVE SUITS THE BOOT

Unless they're well cut with lots of Lycra in the fabric, avoid very tailored trousersuits, which can make you look mannish and shapeless. Jackets should be fitted at the waist to create shape.

WIDE OF THE MARK

Steer clear of wide-legged trousers – they can make your bottom look invisible and hide any shape that you do have. Fitted slim or bootcut are best.

NOT SO HIGH

High-waisted trousers are not the most flattering choice for women of this body shape as they will eliminate curves and make you look even longer than you are.

HOURGLASS FIGURES

YOU'VE AN HOURGLASS FIGURE IF ...

Your waist is narrow but your hips and shoulders are wide. You have a good-sized bust and tend to carry fat equally over your whole body. Your stomach is flat and toned but your thighs have a tendency to look heavy. Use the following tips to maximize your shape ...

TEA FOR TWO

Forties-style tea dresses are made for your figure. Similar to today's shirtdresses, they're wider on the bust and narrow at the waist, curving over the hips and narrowing again at the legs to make the most of your womanly shape.

THIGH DISGUISE

Hide thicker-than-you'd-like thighs under full skirts. Wear with a shirt tied at the waist and a heel to make you look more slender.

THE THIN END ...

Choose thinner belts over wide or you'll look like the proverbial egg timer. Thinner belts flatter without being over-the-top for your figure.

MAKE A CROSSOVER

Dresses or tops that cross over at the waist look good and emphasize a great cleavage. Balance a top with wide-leg trousers and make sure the skirt of the dress is full enough to balance out your shape and prevent you looking top-heavy.

WHAT LIES BENEATH

Invest in good-quality underwear to give your bust and bottom great support. Try sexy seamless shorts and full-figure bras to avoid seams and lines showing through your clothes.

GOT IT? FLAUNT IT

Don't try to hide your body under baggy tops and loose trousers – you'll just look bigger than you are. Make the most of your shape by wearing well-fitting tops and tailored bottoms for everyday elegance.

BOXING CLEVER

Structured cropped jackets and boxy shapes that end on the bottom of the hip add proportion to your top half and draw attention to your narrow waist.

STICK THE BOOT IN

When it comes to choosing the most flattering trouser shape for you, bootcut wins every time as it helps to balance out wider hips. Go for dark denim jeans and black trousers – they will also make your thighs look thinner.

HIDE AND PEEP

Round-toed shoes and peep-toed heels are the best shape of shoe for you: they match the curves of your body and give you a 1950s sex-kitten look.

FAB FORTIES AND FIFTIES

The styles of the 1940s and 1950s are perfect for you. Choose belted jackets and pencil skirts. Opt for tailored styles and stretch fabrics to sculpt and tame your curves. Remember to wear heels to balance heavy thighs and make calves look slim.

THE LONG AND THE SHORT OF IT ...

Very short skirts are not a great idea if you have wide hips and heavy thighs. But if you can't resist, try woollen tights in the same shade as the skirt for a slimming effect.

THE SKINNY ON JEANS

While skinny jeans may be in fashion they do nothing to flatter your shapely figure. The tapered ankle and snug fit will make your hips and thighs look bigger than they are. Wide-leg or bootcut styles work best for you.

PEAR SHAPES

YOU'VE A PEAR SHAPE IF ...

You are small-breasted and have a small waist with curvy, wider hips, a rounded bottom and heavy thighs. You may also have a slender neck and sloping shoulders. Try the following tips to flatter your bottom-heavy shape ...

MIND THE GAP

Hipster trousers are good for getting rid of the gaping waist problem often suffered by small-waisted pear-shapers. Look for low trousers or jeans that sit neatly on the hips and draw attention to a tiny waist.

SHOW OFF YOUR WAIST

Draw attention to your upper body and waist by wearing neat fitted tops with pretty necklines, patterns and colours. Baggy tops will cover your waist instead of highlighting it.

SKIRT AROUND IT

A-line skirts are by far the most flattering style for pear shapes as they slim the hips and emphasize your smaller waist area. Short, tight skirts should be avoided, however, as these will accentuate the tops of your thighs and divert attention to that problematic area below the waist.

CROP FLOPS

Avoid cropped trousers as they can 'cut your legs off' and make them look shorter and your hips and thighs wider.

LUSCIOUS LEGS

If you're wearing boots and you also have heavy thighs, the more fitted and shapely the boots are, the better. They will help to balance you out and make your legs look thinner.

ON THE LINE

Don't wear skirts that are cut on the bias as they will cling to all your lumps and bumps, highlighting tums and bottoms. Skirts with straight lines are the most flattering styles for pear-shaped women.

BALANCE IT OUT

Pear-shaped women characteristically have slimmer shoulders than hips, so even out your shape by picking tops and shirts with puffed sleeves.

WIDE-LEG SAILOR STYLES

Though it may seem that wide legs could make you look larger than you are, you will actually look long and lean in sailor-style wide-legged trousers. They are great for pear shapes as they create a straight line from the hips to the hem.

BELOW THE WAIST

Trousers and skirts with waistlines that sit slightly below the natural waistline flatter pear-shaped hips. Without extra layers close to the smallest part of your waist, you can make it look smaller and your torso seem a little longer.

KNEES UP

Go for dresses and skirts that end just above the knee and in the winter team them with dark-coloured straight boots to hide chunky calves.

IN THE DARK

Dark-coloured trousers with a wide leg suit your shape best as they skim over your heavier bottom and thighs.

APPLE SHAPES

YOU'VE AN APPLE SHAPE IF YOU ...

You have full breasts and a wide back, slim arms and wide shoulders, slim hips and legs plus a small, rounded bottom with a soft, rounded tummy. Make the most of your body shape by using the following tips ...

LOSE THE MUFFIN

Wear shirts that extend lower than your waist to reduce the chances of any 'muffin top' – that is, a roll of flesh escaping between where your shirt meets your trousers. If you like your hips to look a little more in balance with your bust, try a shirt that meets the largest point of the hips.

HANG LOOSE

Try loose, unstructured jackets over slim-fitting dresses to even out your figure.

DON'T BE CLINGY

Choosing the right material for your shape is very important. Don't go for tops created from tight-fitting material such as Lycra, as they will cling to every lump and bump. Tailored clothes made of cotton will always be more flattering on your shape.

HANG LOOSE

Skirts that sit just below the waistline with a brightly coloured belt or band will draw attention away from your waist and highlight your slim hips.

MOVING ON UP

Choose a shirt with a slightly lower neckline to keep the eyes moving upwards. Pair it with a statement necklace for maximum effect.

SKIM IT

Try a thin chiffon blouse over a cotton camisole to skim over a thicker midriff. Wear it open at the neck to highlight your bust.

BE BROAD-MINDED

Look for flowing, wide-legged palazzo trousers – these will create a more even look between your upper and lower halves and also flaunt your slim ankles.

THIN END OF THE WEDGE

Embrace chunkier-style shoes such as wedges. Wearing a slightly heavier shoe can help to anchor and balance your top half.

VERY JANE AUSTEN

The empire line that cinches in just below the bust is a good shape for apples. Try floaty empire-line tops to maximize your cleavage and draw attention away from your waist.

HOT LEGS

Skinny trousers show off your fabulously slim legs and small bottom, but team them with a longer sweater or tunic to help slim your waist.

GO TO GREAT LENGTHS

When buying a trouser suit opt for a longer length jacket rather than a standard length as they can finish at an unflattering angle and draw attention to your tummy.

TIGHT FIT

Keep away from very fitted or tailored suits, particularly those with well-defined waistbands, as they will only draw unwanted attention to your mid-section.

PERFECT YOUR PINS

Wear short skirts with bare legs or flesh-coloured tights to draw attention to your shapely legs.

TROUBLESHOOTING BODY FLAWS

LOSE THOSE LOVE HANDLES

Floaty tops and A-line skirts miraculously hide extra flesh around the hips and waist. Structured clothing such as well-tailored jackets will also help.

VERTICALLY CHALLENGED

Long wide-legged trousers lengthen legs – especially when worn with high boots. Vertical pinstripes and front creases are also flattering if you want to look taller.

FULLER BUST

A sleeveless turtleneck diverts attention away from a busty upper body by emphasizing the arms. Similarly, a cropped jacket draws the eye to the waist. Always wear a bra that fits you properly and has adequate support to lift your boobs.

BIG BOTTOM

A long-line blazer will hide your behind and give you the confidence to wear a body-fitting dress or a pair of straight-leg jeans. Avoid G-strings as they can accentuate a large backside. Choose hipster briefs instead, with plenty of Lycra support to lift your bum and prevent it looking saggy.

WIDE HIPS

Choose A-line skirts in plain colours to minimize wide hips. You should also avoid shiny, satin fabrics or bright-coloured skirts and trousers that will draw attention to saddlebags and create a wider silhouette.

STUBBY LEGS

Shorter skirts make all women look taller but they don't have to be minis: just-above-the-knee will work, too. Avoid longer skirts that make you look as if you are standing in a hole, however.

BROAD SHOULDERS

Soften wide shoulders with cardigans, shrugs and fitted blouses. Avoid jackets and structured suits that will only emphasize angles and make you look wider.

SHORT BOTTOM HALF

Empire-waist dresses will lengthen your lower half. Try above-the-knee lengths as well to keep the look modern.

SHORT BODY

Keep jackets short and sweet – longer jackets will only make you look shorter.

BINGO WINGS

Cover less-than-slender arms in draped bell sleeves and light floaty fabrics. Resist the urge to wear bulky sweaters – they just make your arms look bigger.

FLAT BUM

Invest in some shaper support knickers to lift and give your bottom shape. Hipster jeans create the illusion of a small rounded bottom and add shape where there isn't any.

WIDE BOTTOM

Straight wide-legged trousers even out a wide bottom, especially when teamed with a fitted top and jacket.

SHORT NECK

The ultimate lengthening trick is to wear the 'Sabrina' neckline – named after Audrey Hepburn's character in the film of the same name. It's a wide, shallow, straight neckline, sometimes called a 'boatneck', and was created by Hubert de Givenchy, who designed many of Hepburn's clothes.

SPECIAL OCCASION DRESSING

CASUAL DAYWEAR

CASUAL, NOT SCRUFFY

Don't skimp on the quality of casual clothes. Cheap fabrics look cheap and will deteriorate very quickly. Stick to 100% cottons, wools and silks with a little added Lycra to keep the shape and allow the garment some 'give'.

THE LONG AND SHORT OF IT

Don't wear sweaters that are too long over jeans if you're short – they'll only make you look smaller. Instead, try a fitted lamb's wool cardigan over a camisole or a shaped v-neck or polo.

STEAL CONTINENTAL STYLE

Classic, fitted open-necked shirts with a knotted scarf at the neck worn with jeans and boots or flats will take you anywhere with effortless chic. Dress the look up with a blazer or down with a cashmere sweater.

EASE YOURSELF INTO CASUAL

If you still prefer to wear suits for work and find it hard to dress down, liven the tailoring up with unexpected high-impact jewellery and funky shoes.

IT'S A WRAP

For an all-purpose, wear anywhere, anytime outfit, a wrap dress is a great investment. Pick one in jersey fabric that drapes gracefully and will flatter almost every figure. Try a small geometric print for a modern look or invest in a solid colour that will work for evening, too.

ACCESSORIZE RIGHT

Don't wear sparkly jewellery or anything too big with casual clothes – it will look bling-heavy. Keep it small and understated so you don't look as if you've tried too hard.

HAVE A PLAN

Buy your casual clothes in the same way as you choose career clothes. Don't just buy random comfy tops and bottoms, pick cohesive pieces and build them around basic styles. A good approach is three colours for the best mix-and-match wardrobe – khaki, denim and cream, or black, khaki and white. You can then throw colourful tops and accessories into the mix.

GET THE COAT RIGHT

Don't ruin your look with a great big, shapeless coat. Invest in a short, shapely pea coat or a shaped parka. Sleeveless jackets look good with warm lamb's wool or cashmere sweaters. A cosy duffel coat in a pastel colour always looks pretty, too.

FLIP-ING COOL

Look on-trend in the summer by teaming cute floral dresses with flip-flops. Your feet will stay cool and you can carry off the casual shoe style if the rest of your outfit looks groomed.

PERFECT FIT

Just because it's casual, this doesn't mean that big and baggy is OK. Even if it's simply a tracksuit or cotton trousers and a T-shirt, you will feel and look better if everything fits properly. If you really love oversized sweaters, make sure you team them with a belt and keep the trousers skinny.

LAYERS ARE KEY

Effortless, relaxed dressing style is down to good layering. Camisoles under shirts or with a wrap cardie look great, as do long-sleeved T-shirts underneath short-sleeved tees in toning colours. A draped cardigan and well-cut jeans with a scarf will take you anywhere.

SMART-CASUAL

DON A BLAZER

Need to smarten up a casual outfit in a hurry? Pulling on this wardrobe staple adds a touch of class to everything from simple white blouses to plain black trousers and jeans.

BE A YUMMY MUMMY

For school concerts and parents' evenings you can't beat a smart-casual look. You want to look sensible but not matronly so opt for chic linen trousers instead of jeans and knee-length skirts rather than minis.

GET A BEADED CLUTCH

Even for daytime, a stylish handbag adds panache to your special occasion ensemble. Invest in an all-purpose clutch decorated with subtle beading (avoid sequins and glitter, which are not so classic). But be sure it's big enough to hold a wallet, lipstick and keys.

ON THE JOB

JUST THE JOB

First impressions are very important so make sure your future employer is not put off at first glance. You want to look smart and organized but not dull and dismal. Think chic trousers or skirt, an interesting shirt and a fitted long cardigan or jacket in similar, subtle colours.

SHOW YOUR PERSONALITY

While it's important to look together and groomed you should also reveal a touch of your personality to a potential employer to ensure you stand out from all the rest. Think about an unusual belt, brooch or beaded necklace to add a touch of individuality to your outfit.

IMPRESSING AT INTERVIEW

Do your research! Find out how formal the company is. However, even if the staff wear jeans from day to day, it's always better to attend an interview wearing something smarter.

BE SUIT-ABLY ATTIRED

A classic trouser suit is worth investing a bit of money in – it should last a few years. The better the quality of the fabric and lining, the better the investment. A good suit can be the most wearable outfit you own as it can be dressed up or down, the jacket can be worn separately with jeans and the trousers or skirt with shirts.

OFFICE TO EVENING

A SUITABLE STYLE

If you have to wear a suit to work, try choosing one that you can carry off easily from day to night. Go for a style that breaks from the norm or is in a colour other than black. A well-cut suit in a unique design can also be pieced separately, such as with a pair of smart jeans that you can then wear straight to the bar.

THE CLASSIC LBD

The little black dress is a versatile item that you can wear from office to evening. Wear to the office with flats and a chunky-knit cardigan and belt, then change into heels, add some jewellery and leave the cardigan in the cloakroom for an instantly glamorous evening look.

SEXY CLUTCHES

Don't let a huge workbag ruin your evening look. Leave anything you don't need in your drawer at work and take out just the essentials in a smart and sexy clutch bag.

PARTY & FORMAL

COCKTAIL HOUR

For black-tie and cocktail parties the look to go for is chic and poised. The hemline on the dress is not of such importance – but the width certainly is. Keep it streamlined and well cut instead of billowing and flouncy.

DRESS FOR BLACK TIE

A floor-length smart cocktail frock in a dark shade is great to have in your wardrobe as a fail-safe choice for black-tie events. Go for a classic cut to which you can add accessories and different pairs of shoes to bring it bang up-to-date each time you wear it.

GO TO MAXI LENGTHS

Many women are wary of long dresses but they are an easy way to get instant evening glamour, whether you're going to a ball or society event or attending the theatre or ballet. Team with simple accessories and an elegant clutch bag – and don't forget the heels!

BIRTHDAY BEAUTY

If it's your birthday you want to make sure you look your best. Plan in advance and treat yourself to something special. If you're going for a meal, remember you'll be sitting down most of the night, so make the most of a pretty top and statement jewellery.

AT-HOME STYLE

CHIC BUT COMFY

Casual jeans or a skirt with a glamorous top and shoes are great for entertaining at home, and can look artlessly elegant when accessorized with good jewellery.

CHECK IT FIRST

You will be getting up and down quite a lot if you're the host, so make sure you don't wear something that shifts around, exposes flesh, rides up or creases easily.

ACCESSORIZE WISELY

Wear a scarf around your head or to secure a ponytail to keep your hair out of the way, but avoid long sleeves or scarves that may prove to be a safety hazard in the kitchen!

DATE CLOTHES

BE COMFORTABLE

Don't squeeze into something that doesn't fit or wear clothes that are not your style. You'll feel awkward and be concentrating on your outfit more than the flow of conversation.

BE YOURSELF

Try wearing something that reflects your personality, such as a favourite bracelet or a quirky handbag. Not only will you feel more comfortable but this will also help your date to know a bit more about you.

CHOOSE SHOES CAREFULLY

Make sure your shoes match your outfit and are suitable for your date – but most importantly, make sure you feel comfortable in them. You want to be enjoying the romance and not focusing on your sore feet.

DON'T EXPERIMENT!

Wear garments and accessories in shapes and colours that you know you already look good in. He's not to know just how old your most flattering top is.

PHONE A FRIEND

Ask a trusted friend for advice on your date outfit. They will be able to give you their honest opinion and save you from any embarrassment.

DON'T DRESS DOWN

Dress up slightly more than you would to meet a friend for a date. Not only will this mean that you won't end up looking too casual but it will also show your date that you have made an effort and that you are interested in him.

STYLISH SMALLS

While your date might not get to see it, wearing lingerie that matches and fits well will give you inner confidence and an extra touch of sexiness.

EASE UP ON KILLER HEELS

If your date is on the diminutive side you don't want to intimidate him by towering over him in your stilettos. And even tall men like to feel they tower over you a bit – it brings out their protective side!

TRIED AND TESTED

You can never fail with the trusty LBD. Add your favourite jewellery, scarf or bag to tie in with the location of your date and to show off your individuality.

STAND UP STRAIGHT!

Whatever you're wearing you will always look better if you have great posture. Stand with your shoulders back and your head held high and you'll instantly look and feel thinner and more confident.

DON'T GO IN DISGUISE

Dress for yourself first and your date after. If the first meeting goes well, you don't want to feel forced to wear clothes that are not really you every time you get together.

ACCENTUATE THE LESS OBVIOUS

The neck, shoulders and back are some of the parts of the body that men find most alluring in women. Try a strapless top or a dress with a low back for a hint of sexiness without showing off too much skin.

LET YOUR PERSONALITY DO THE TALKING

Never let your clothes overpower what's beneath them. Wouldn't you rather your date remembered you for your great personality and sparkling eyes than because of your amazing Mulberry handbag?

CHECK THE FORECAST

Organize an alternative outfit in the event of unreliable weather. You don't want to be left shivering in a light cotton sundress during a summer shower. Additionally, be careful with white articles of clothing if you have to travel in the rain as they can easily become transparent when wet.

IF ALL ELSE FAILS …

Your favourite jeans with heels and a pretty top and blazer-style jacket is always a safe compromise that works for most situations.

FUNERALS & WEDDINGS

A SIGN OF RESPECT

Always ask about the dress code before going to a funeral. Sometimes people are asked to wear the deceased's favourite colour or not to wear black. If this is not the case, then black, navy or dark brown is the safest option. Go for smart, tailored knee-length skirts and fitted jackets. A soft, beige-coloured pashmina can break up the look. The main rule is to look smart and respectful.

NEVER UPSTAGE THE BRIDE

While you want to look your best at weddings, always remember that the bride should be the centre of attention, not you. Avoid wearing any real statement pieces or anything too flouncy and don't wear white unless it's the background colour to a pattern.

IN TUNE WITH THE SEASONS

As a general rule for a special event, try to match the colour of your clothes to the shade of the season. Darker berry colours mixed with blacks and greys work well in winter, while pastels are great during the summer. For autumn, think browns, greens and oranges, and opt for pretty pinks and purples in springtime.

FEATHER IN YOUR CAP

Instead of hats, look for large hair clips or statement headpieces made from feathers or bows for a more modern look. But remember, the fancier you go on top, the simpler your outfit below should be.

CHECK THE INVITE

Dress up more for weddings after 6 pm and keep things a bit more relaxed for morning and afternoon affairs. If the wedding is in the morning and the reception takes place in the evening, dress for the latter – the church service will be over more quickly than the reception and you don't want to feel uncomfortable all evening.

BUY A FABULOUS COAT

If you are attending a winter wedding, don't ruin your amazing outfit with a dull coat. Go for frock coats in a block colour that tones with your outfit or pick one with a great pattern.

QUICK COVER-UP

For a summer wedding, strappy dresses can look great but make sure you bring along a shawl or little cardigan to cover your shoulders in case the weather turns colder.

CHRISTENINGS

BABY BLUES

Christenings can be tricky to dress for. You want to look smart but not too 'wedding'. Think knee-length skirts and pretty sweaters or smart trousers with detailed shirts and tailored jackets.

WEAR THE RIGHT HEEL

Remember that at a christening you may be expected to hold the baby at some point, so wear shoes that you can stand safely in and which won't cause you to topple over!

OUTDOOR EVENTS

DRESS TO THE MAX

For summer evening events where you'll be eating al fresco, stand out in style with a floor-length maxi dress. Choose from fitted to floaty, and spaghetti-straps to thicker halter-neck ties, and team with a cute cardigan.

ROUGH AND TUMBLE

Jeans are perfect for outdoor parties. They're sexy, practical for dancing or games, they don't show grass or food stains easily and smart designer jeans are accepted pretty much anywhere. Team them with a glamorous summery top so you still look like you've made an effort.

PRACTICAL CHOICE

T-dresses may not seem the obvious choice for festivals but they are very versatile. Wear them over jeans for one look and with cowboy boots for another. Go for those with sleeves to protect your shoulders from burning in the sunshine. And don't forget a stylish raincoat for any wet days.

OUTDOOR ENTERTAINMENT

When attending an outdoor concert or play, think comfort and layers. If it takes place on a warm summer's afternoon, leading into a chillier evening, try dark linen trousers or wide knee-length skirts (so you can sit on the ground comfortably) with a camisole, cotton top and wrap cardigan.

WEAR A HAT TO BANISH BAD HAIR

Dirty hair is always a problem on camping holidays and at outdoor festivals, so make sure you pack a great summer hat to keep it hidden. Choose a straw cowboy hat or a floppy hat during the day, then swap it for a dark-coloured beanie in the evening.

A DAY AT THE RACEs

Dressing up for the races is essential, but remember to keep your choices elegant and ladylike. If you'd wear it out to a nightclub or a formal ball, it's not the right choice!

PICK ONE FABULOUS ITEM

For those on a budget, work your look around one amazing item such as a hat, shoes or a dress that flatters your best feature and keep everything else low-key.

STUCK IN THE MUD

While strappy sandals may go perfectly with your dress, think about how they will cope on grass if the event is outdoors, especially if it's a little muddy. Go for a more structured heel or wedges so you don't sink into the ground.

MEET & GREETS

IMPRESSING THE IN-LAWS

Whether it's the first time you meet them or the twentieth, save the revealing outfits for your partner and cover up for his parents. You don't need to change your style, just check whether all that flesh really needs to be on show before you leave the house!

DON'T BE BOLD

Avoid flashy or aggressive colours such as red and black and opt instead for a softer taupe or pewter that will make you appear nonthreatening, calm and approachable. Inject colour with a bright necklace or scarf.

REUNIONS

IMPRESS OLD CLASSMATES

The important thing is to feel confident when you dress for a class reunion. Plan ahead so you feel comfortable in what you are wearing. Look through your wardrobe for outfits that you know you look good in, then add up-to-the-minute accessories.

DRESS YOUR AGE

While you want to look gorgeous for your 'friends or classmates reunited' get-together, don't dress too young – even if you last saw these people 25 years ago! Skintight or too short will look ridiculous; besides, you want them to see how you've grown into a sophisticated, successful adult.

SEASONAL HOLIDAYS

AVOID FESTIVE FAUX PAS

If you're acting as hostess for Christmas dinner, be sure to glam it up while still keeping things practical. You are bound to be on your feet quite often so swap your heels for jewelled or satin flats and keep your sleeves three-quarter length so they don't end up trailing in the gravy.

DANCING QUEEN

New Year's Eve only happens once a year so make sure you look your best. There's bound to be some dancing involved so go for a stunning dress that lets you move easily and twirl around freely.

GREET NEW YEAR ON YOUR FEET

A New Year's Eve party usually involves a long evening on your feet, so make sure your shoes are comfy. Of course you still want to look glamorous with a pair of heels – but they don't have to be your highest pair. You want to be able to dance and not worry about falling over after a few glasses of champagne!

PERFECT PINS

The last evening of the year is all about having fun so do the same with your clothes. You could contrast a block-colour dress with brightly coloured tights – or if you are feeling brave, try teaming a black dress with a pair of bright red or purple tights.

TRAVEL FASHION

SET THE SCENE

Good packing is all in the planning. Be realistic about what you need – consider the climate, how long you will be away and exactly what kind of holiday it's going to be.

DOWNSIZE YOUR PURSE

You don't need to take your normal purse with its backlog of receipts, reminders and photos on holiday. Treat yourself to a new, minimal wallet that will fit your money and the necessary cards inside, allowing more space in your bag for souvenirs.

ADOPT A THEME

Pack clothes that you can mix and match rather than items that only go with one outfit. This will save on packing space and also on washing when you get back. To avoid creasing, layer each outfit as flat as possible with tissue paper between the folds to limit creases, and in order of what you think you might wear first.

CHECK THE WEATHER

It sounds obvious but check the weather forecast for the place you are visiting on the Internet before you pack so that you have an idea of what to expect. Look up the average temperature and rainfall for the time of year you're going, too.

PASSPORT POWER

Apart from the tickets, your passport is the most important thing about your trip, so give it a well-deserved makeover with a special passport cover. Choose a leather case in a colour that coordinates with your handbag to get your holiday off to a stylish start.

STEAM CLEAN

If your clothes are crumpled after being in your suitcase, hang them up in the bathroom while you have a shower and the steam will make the creases disappear effortlessly. For wrinkled jumpers, aim a hot hairdryer at the creases and they will soon drop out.

BAG IT UP

Pack your delicate underwear in lingerie bags and keep each pair of shoes in a separate shoebag. Not only will this help your packing be organized, but you will protect your lingerie and keep it from getting tangled up with other items of clothing.

CROSS YOUR HEART

An across-the-body handbag is a much more practical choice than a shoulder bag when you're on holiday. Not only does it free up your hands, it will also deter pickpockets – a huge problem in lots of tourist destinations.

STREAMLINE YOUR SUITCASE

A couple of days before your trip, lay out the clothes you want to take and look through them carefully. Often you can downsize the amount you have at the start by a third or even half.

BE PREPARED

Pack a spare set of underwear and socks into your hand luggage just in case your suitcase goes missing.

MAKE LIKE A LOCAL

Be sure to respect local customs on clothing when visiting countries of different cultures, and pack accordingly. For example, if you're travelling to a Muslim country or plan to visit lots of churches and religious buildings, wear below-the-knee dresses or trousers and have a scarf or shawl handy to cover up your shoulders.

DEVELOP SUITCASE CHIC

Battered old luggage will let you down. Look for cases made of good-quality material in stylish colours that coordinate with your outfit.

DRESS UP FOR THE PLANE

On the plane, wear your heaviest clothes such as jeans, boots and an overcoat to save much-needed space in your suitcase.

PLANE-CLOTHED

Make sure you wear comfortable clothing on your flight, especially for longer journeys. Planes are often colder than you expect, so think layers and take a pair of cosy cashmere socks. Check that your shoes are not too tight as your feet may swell due to the cabin pressure, and pack a pashmina, which you can use instead of scratchy plane blankets.

CASE-SHARE

If you are going away with friends, check what they are packing. You may be able to borrow each others' clothes and designate certain items to pack to one another so that you don't end up with four hairdryers and four bottles of shampoo plus conditioner.

GET SOME SHUT-EYE

If you have an overnight flight, treat yourself to a pretty eye mask that will assist you in getting a stylish forty winks on the plane and a rested, fresh complexion when you land.

HOT-WEATHER HOLIDAYS

ROMAN HOLIDAY

Keep your basic flip-flops for the beach and look for smarter sandals for the evening. The gladiator sandal is a stylish alternative that will look fabulous with a tan and dress and equally good with trousers or shorts.

DRESS IT UP

For a summer holiday always pack a couple of versatile sundresses that you can slip on over a swimsuit, wear for sightseeing during the day, and then smarten up with some jewellery and little heels in the evening.

WET SUITS

Take separate swim bags to keep swimsuits and bikinis in – especially if you might have to carry them about when they're wet. Pack a small sachet of detergent to rinse them in to prevent chlorine or salt build-up over the holiday period.

ALL THAT GLITTERS

Gold looks fantastic against a great tan so pack some gold jewellery or clothes for a sexy Latino look that maximizes tanned skin and sun-glistened hair.

THE RIGHT SHADES

Sunglasses are an essential – but with so many shapes, sizes and colours on offer it's worth spending a bit of time to find the perfect pair. Ask a friend to give you their honest opinion. And make sure your shades protect against UVB and UVA rays. Polarized lenses protects the eyes from glare, sun and UV radiation, and don't distort colour.

PALE AND INTERESTING

Save your light-coloured bikinis and white dresses for the last few days of your holiday when you have built up more of a tan, otherwise they may leave you looking washed-out in the bright sun.

GOOD SUPPORT

Padded bikinis are not only fantastic for offering support on the beach but can also double up as bras for the evening, saving you valuable space in your suitcase.

TONE IT DOWN

If you've over-done the sun, avoid wearing bright colours, which will highlight your red, burning skin. Stick to pale shades and use a cardigan or pashmina to cover sunburnt shoulders.

COVERED TO A T

If your shoulders are prone to burning, keep a couple of T-shirts in your bag that you can throw on at the beach or while sightseeing to protect your skin.

SUNCREAM SAVVY

Even when you're in a rush to get out and about during the day, make sure your sun cream or aftersun is dry before dressing to avoid getting marks on your clothing.

COLOURED UP

Be brave with colour. If you always wear darker shades at home, a sunny location offers the perfect opportunity to experiment with bright shades without feeling as if you're standing out too much from the crowd. Bold colour looks fantastic against tanned skin.

MAXED-OUT

Long summer maxi-dresses are great for an effortless boho look in the evenings. Choose styles with thin straps to show off your tanned shoulders and back.

COLD-WEATHER HOLIDAYS

LAYER IT ON THICK
If you are going on a winter city break, packing layers – such as long-sleeved T-shirts, cashmere cardigans and pashminas – is the best way to ensure you stay warm without having to take your biggest, heaviest sweaters.

CHOOSE COATS WITH CARE
For winter city breaks, a warm and fabulous coat is a must. It's your one chance to exude style while the rest of your clothes are covered up. Choose a striking scarf, hat and glove combo for extra fashion points.

LONG ICED-TS
On a winter vacation, take a variety of long-sleeved T-shirts in various bright colours. They are incredibly versatile and can be worn under short-sleeved tops, sweaters or the jacket of a suit.

CITY & WEEKEND BREAKS

WEEKEND WARDROBE
For weekends away, aim for a capsule wardrobe that is easy to coordinate – and light to carry! Two dresses, one pair of trousers, two tops and a light sweater should be plenty. You can add accessories at night for colour and style.

GO FLAT-HUNTING

Comfortable shoes are a must for weekend and city breaks filled with sightseeing. Flat ballet-style pumps look great and are very practical. Wear new shoes around the house for a few days before your trip so you don't get blisters.

DITCH THE SUITCASE

If you're only going away for a couple of days, pack all your items in a small suitcase to carry as hand luggage. By doing this you can spend less time waiting at the airport and more time enjoying your trip.

DEAL WITH DIFFERENT TEMPERATURES

Pack a cotton long-sleeved top in your bag for walking around warm foreign cities so you can cover up while visiting chillier air-conditioned buildings or churches.

PREGNANCY STYLE

PUT YOUR FEET UP

When you're pregnant, the last thing you want to do is haul yourself around shops to find clothes. Do this from the comfort of your own home. There are dozens of great maternity-wear websites that deliver gorgeous pregnancy outfits direct to your door.

GET SOME LAYERS

Try layering simple camisoles with chiffon over tops in accompanying colours for a chic and pretty look that will keep you cool on summer days while flattering your bump.

BALANCE IT OUT

Because the tops you will be wearing have to 'grow', avoid feeling like you're wearing a tent by ensuring your bottom half is more streamlined. Look for slim-legged pregnancy jeans to minimize your overall volume.

PRETTY FLATS

With swollen ankles and that extra baby weight, cute flat shoes are a must for pregnant women. Treat yourself to a couple of pairs in different fabrics so you can wear them to formal and informal occasions.

BUY ONE SIZE UP

Maternity clothes aren't compulsory in the early months, especially if it's only your tummy that's grown – just buy a size bigger. You can then wear the same stretchy dresses, tops and shirts after the birth while losing your baby weight.

WORKING MUM

Looking chic in the office while pregnant can become a challenge. To make it easy, create a capsule wardrobe with a pair of smart trousers with an elasticated or drawstring waistband, a skirt, a jacket you can wear open, a dress and a tunic top. They can be mixed and matched to create different looks and should see you through in style.

STICK TO YOUR FAVOURITE STORES

Being pregnant doesn't mean you should avoid the shops you love best. Many of the major high-street stores have fantastic maternity collections mirroring up-to-the-minute trends.

SHOW OFF YOUR CURVES

V-neck tops and scoop-neck tops in empire lines will flatter an ever-growing cleavage and prevent you from looking large on top.

GET SOME SUPPORT

Your bust will grow at least a cup size when pregnant so it's important to get bras that fit your size and offer great support – your local department store should be able to help. And remember to have yourself measured properly for a nursing bra just a few weeks before the birth if you plan to breastfeed.

SOME EXTRA STRETCH

One sneaky trick that will allow you to carry on wearing your favourite pair of trousers in the first few months of pregnancy is to loop an elastic band through the button-hole and hook it around the button. Make sure you disguise it by wearing a long shirt over the top, though.

SORT OUT SIZING

Always select your pre-pregnancy size when buying maternity clothes. After all, your arms and legs don't get longer and your basic body structure will remain the same. Well-made maternity garments adjust for pregnancy, giving you extra room only where you need it – belly, bust and hips – while maintaining the pre-pregnancy proportions of each size range.

SOMETHING BORROWED …

Who wants to spend money on clothes they may never wear again? Instead of paying out for a whole pregnancy wardrobe, borrow items from friends who have already had their babies or hunt for bargains in charity shops.

BEAUTIFULLY WRAPPED

Wrap-around dresses and tops are a great choice for soon-to-be mums as the v-neck front will flatter your chest and the tied waist allows for the growth of your bump. Choose one or two sizes bigger than you normally are to allow for give.

SHOW OFF YOUR SLIM BITS

If you are pregnant but haven't put on much weight anywhere else, don't be afraid to display your best features such as shoulders and arms in off-the-shoulder dresses. Being pregnant doesn't mean you can't look sexy. Quite the opposite, in fact.

RECYCLE OLD TROUSERS

Most women have a couple of pairs of linen trousers or cargo pants lurking in their wardrobes from the summer so instead of buying new trousers, reuse these. If the waistbands aren't drawstring, leave the waistband undone and loop a thick belt over the top. Team with a long cotton top.

BE BIAS

Dresses cut on the bias will have more give than straight-cut styles and are the perfect choice when your bump is getting bigger.

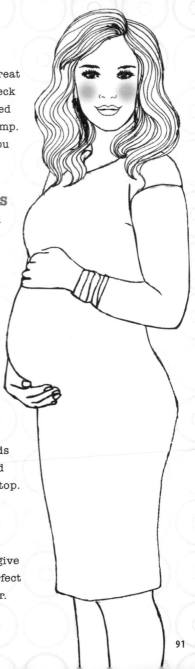

SHOW OFF YOUR SHAPE

Define your figure by choosing long floaty tops with ties that do up under the bust or at the side. For glamorous evening events, add a thick ribbon or a belt to shapeless tops under the bust and above the bump.

GET GOOD COVER

Short-sleeved cardigans and cowls that hang loosely to the waist are great for keeping you warm on summer evenings and flattering your bump.

GYM & SPORTSWEAR

AND STRETCH ...

Gym clothes should allow you to move freely. Look for materials that have some extra stretch in them so you don't feel restricted and unable to twist into that tricky yoga pose!

YOGA MATTERS

By spending a bit extra on well-made and flattering yoga bottoms, not only will you look good in class, but you can also wear them for a stylish yet relaxed look around the house.

AVOID SWEAT MARKS

Minimize sweat marks by looking out for specially designed sports clothes that are made of 'wicking' fabric, such as high-tech polyester, which draws sweat away from the body. While items made of this breathable fabric are a little more expensive, they'll keep you comfortable and dry.

A GOOD FIT

A big mistake that many women make in the gym is to wear overly baggy clothes – but this actually makes them look larger. The most flattering fitness clothes are those that follow the shape of your body and give you a waist.

USE LAYERS

If you're exercising outside, the best way to deal with changes in body temperature is thin layers. A strappy vest under a thin long-sleeved top with a thin zip-up means you can add or discard items as you go.

DON'T GO BUST

The right bra is essential for exercising, especially if your breasts are big. Go to a sports shop to find a well-designed bra that will lift, hold and separate. Opt for feel over look – bouncing, unsupported boobs are uncomfortable and bad for your back.

SECRET SUPPORT

Built-in support on vest tops in well-designed fitness clothing means you can show off toned arms and shoulders while keeping everything else in place.

IT ONLY TAKES TWO

Having at least two great-looking gym outfits that flatter your figure and make you feel good will give you extra incentive to go to the gym and show off your sleek, chic look.

PLAY IT SAFE IN BLACK

Black is the most flattering of colours and great to wear to the gym if you feel self-conscious about your figure. Add some colour by choosing black trousers with piping or waistbands in a different shade.

DON'T FORGET TO ACCESSORIZE

Just because you're working out doesn't mean you can't wear cool accessories. Forget jewellery and try coloured sweatbands or hair bands to keep your hair out of your eyes.

SHOPPING

PLANNING AHEAD

WRITE A LIST
Before you go out shopping for clothes write down a list of exactly what you're looking for – and stick to it. This will save you money because you won't be distracted by other items that you don't really need.

TAKE IT WITH YOU
If you have a skirt that you love but have never found anything to wear it with, or maybe a top that none of your bottoms quite match, pop it in a bag and take it out shopping. Make it your mission to find the perfect partner.

BE A LONE BROWSER
Shopping on your own is quicker and you won't get sidetracked. If you really need a second opinion, you can always try the garment on at home and ask someone but make sure the shop offers returns first.

HAVE A 'SHOPPING' OUTFIT
Wear clothes that are easy to take on and off without making you look like a rumpled mess by the end of the day. Streamlined but supportive underwear won't spoil the look of any clothes you try on. And do your hair and make-up so you see yourself in the best light.

PRIORITIZE PURCHASES

What's the most important purchase you want to make? If you won't feel satisfied unless you go home with the perfect coat, don't allow yourself to be distracted by other items until you've found it.

FIX YOUR PRICE

Set a limit on how much you can spend and be firm: do not allow yourself to go over that figure. If you know you can't control yourself once you see something you like, leave your credit and store cards at home. Try taking cash instead, as it feels more 'real'. It's also a lot harder to hand over crisp notes than a piece of plastic and this will really test whether you want that new dress as much as you think!

GET YOUR UNDIES RIGHT

Go shopping in the lingerie you expect to wear under the outfit you're buying. It's no good wearing a red bra and panties if you're out looking for a cream cotton summer dress. Similarly, take a pair of tights if you intend to try on a new skirt or dress.

SENSIBLE SHOPPING

JUST WON'T WASH?

Check the washing instructions on the label. Does the item seem quite so desirable if you're going to have to hand-wash or dry-clean it after every wear?

WHEN I'M THINNER ...

Don't put off making wardrobe choices until you lose weight – choose pieces that can camouflage problem areas instead.

AVOID RETAIL AS THERAPY

Don't shop when you're feeling down. You will end up buying mistake items or being overcritical of yourself – both of which can make you feel worse. See a film, take some exercise or meet a friend for lunch for a more effective pick-me-up.

THREE CRUCIAL QUESTIONS

Ask yourself these three questions before you buy anything. Does it fit? Will it go with what I already have? And does it suit me?

IN THE CHANGING ROOM

BE REALISTIC

Just because it looks great on the shop assistant, this doesn't mean it will look equally good on you. She could have an entirely different body shape and colouring – so always try things on before buying and make sure they suit your frame and hair and skin tones.

SIT IT OUT

Always sit down in an item of clothing when trying it on. What may fit while standing can pull or gape open once you sit down and ruin the shape of a garment completely.

WALK THIS WAY

Take a walk in your outfit before you buy it. Many skirts and dresses can look perfect when you are standing still, only to ride up once you walk along. The waistband of your skirt should be large enough so that it doesn't pucker or roll up.

GIVE YOURSELF A 360

Always check the fit of what you are about to buy in a three-way mirror so you can see yourself from every angle. This prevents you getting a nasty surprise when you catch a glimpse of your backside in a shop window at some point in the future!

GETTING A GOOD FIT

DON'T SQUEEZE IN

When buying jackets and coats, remember that the sleeves should just hit the wrist bone and the fabric mustn't cling to or stretch over any problem areas.

HEEL, GIRL!

Trouser bottoms should rest about 2.5 cm (1 in) above the heel and the hems should sit slightly bent on the top of your feet – have one 'break' in the crease. If you're wearing high heels, trousers should be longer to account for the extra height.

GET THE BENDS

Make sure you can bend your arms without difficulty when you try on tops and jackets. Bend your knees, too. Anything too tight or chafing will hurt you and also damage the clothing.

MADE TO MEASURE

Many shop-bought jackets are too wide across the shoulders. A good tailor or seamstress should be able to take them in from the centre seam to fit you perfectly.

KEEP YOUR TROUSERS ON

Check that any new trousers don't have too much fabric in the zipper and crotch – this can make them bunch unattractively.

CH-CH-CH-CHANGES

Invest in good alterations if something doesn't fit or if you lose or gain weight – clothing that doesn't fit properly will never leave your wardrobe.

UP YOUR SLEEVE

Jacket sleeves should be slim to show off the shape of the arms but loose enough to allow you to wear a thin sweater underneath. The bottom of the jacket must hit the hipbones – any shorter or longer tends to make people look squat and bulky.

TUCK IT IN

A good tailored shirt should fit neatly around your torso and be long enough to tuck in – and stay tucked in. Don't buy shirts that scrimp on fabric at the bottom: you'll only end up looking like an unmade bed as the day goes on.

CREATURE COMFORTS

Clothes should never be too painful to wear! Any garments that cut you in half, give you tummy pains, cut off circulation or make you feel faint should be ditched, no matter how gorgeous or glam. You're damaging your health!

AVOID A SQUEEZE

Lycra added to garments is no excuse for you to go a size smaller – jeans and jackets should still fit properly. The elastic simply means that the clothes move with and fit your body more easily and so are more comfortable to wear.

THE RIGHT BUTTONS

Check where the buttons sit on your shirt. A good fit means the neck isn't too low or too high and when open-necked, the top button should sit just above the bust.

GETTING A BARGAIN

IS THE PRICE RIGHT?

By law, shops have to display the original price of the item on sale and it has to have been for sale at this price for at least 28 days. If it doesn't have this information, staff are obliged to tell you so you know whether you're really getting a bargain.

STICK TO CLASSICS

That orange and blue miniskirt might be very this season but how will it look this time next year? During sales you're better off sticking to simple, timeless pieces.

THINK COMFORT

When buying, remember that anything that feels uncomfortable when you first try it on will be murder by the end of the day!

BE FIRM

Decide what you're looking for and stick to it. Don't allow yourself to become sidetracked by price cuts. That cheap dress isn't a bargain if you never wear it.

NO SALE

Don't be drawn in by the price in red. To pass the test, it has to fit, go with at least two items in your wardrobe and have the 'wow' factor.

NET A BARGAIN

Before you shop, check online to see what's on sale in the store to save joining the scrum for nothing! You can even order from the comfort of your armchair to save you that trip into town.

IS IT WORTH IT?

Try this value trick. When you're putting on your bargain top or dress, ask yourself if you love it so much that you'd happily pay full price. If the answer's no, think twice before you buy.

GET STOCKED UP

At sale time, stock up on basics – cotton panties, socks, tights, white shirts, black trousers, neutral shoes, etc.

FEELING BLUE

Many of the big department stores have 'blue cross' sale days where they cut their prices for a few days only. Find out when these dates are due and wait until then to stock up on new clothes on the cheap.

BUDGET BOUTIQUES

Those pricy boutique clothing stores that are normally beyond your price range often do amazing reductions on clothes at sale times, frequently cutting prices by more than 70 per cent. You may still be paying normal high street prices but you'll also be buying designer pieces that are longer-lasting and will look fabulous on. Go just before the end of any sale for even more incredible reductions.

LUXE LINGERIE FOR LESS

Many of the large department stores have designer underwear that is also reduced during annual sales. Visit on the first few days of the sale when there will be more sizes available – the most common sizes are soon snapped up.

A LITTLE LUXE

Now is the time to buy very high-quality items. Good-quality leather boots, handbags and shoes at sale prices are a great investment and will last for years.

SHOP AROUND

To avoid spending unnecessary cash, ask shop assistants to hold items that you are interested in while you continue your search. Most will be happy to put clothes on hold until the next day. After a cooling-off period you can objectively decide whether that hot-pink skirt is such a good buy after all.

MAKE USE OF OFFERS

Often high-street stores have 'three for two' offers in which you can buy a basic shirt or vest top in bulk at a discount. Take advantage of this to stock up on basics.

MONEY-SAVING FASHION

BE A BRIDGET JONES

Keep a diary and write down every single penny you spend for a month. You'll be astonished at how much goes on nonessentials – lunch, chocolate, lattes, etc. – and it soon adds up. Save cash by taking a packed lunch to work and have up to £100 ($200) extra per month to spend on clothes or shoes!

VOUCH FOR IT

Look out for those 15% and 20% money-off vouchers for high-street stores that often come free with magazines. Save serious cash by using them at the beginning of the season when you need to make big purchases such as a coat or pair of boots.

DON'T BE A 10% VICTIM

Research shows we only ever wear 10% of our entire wardrobe. So before buying anything new, ask yourself that difficult question: 'Do I really need another pair of shoes or is there something in the unused 90% of my wardrobe that I can fall in love with again?'

FIX YOUR PRICE

If you're on the lookout for a new outfit but are also restricted to a budget, take with you only the amount of money you want to spend so there's no possibility of you blowing your budget.

WORTH PER WEAR

When it comes to deciding what to buy, think realistically about how often you will wear something. If it's a decision between one expensive item and two cheaper ones, you may find that in reality you end up wearing the more expensive garment more often and actually save yourself more money in the long run, rather than buying cheaper clothes that soon date.

SELL, SELL, SELL!

Use eBay and car boot (garage) sales to buy and sell clothes. Some people actually make a living these days from buying and selling online. You can sell almost anything for the price of a small commission. And garage sales are fantastic for making money out of junk – it's amazing what people will buy!

USE WEB DISCOUNTS

Sign up to online discount services (such as www.vouchercodes. co.uk) to learn about discounts currently on offer on a whole range of clothes. They will also send you up-to-date money-off vouchers and details of offers available at stores and online.

SPLIT THE COST

If you and your friends have a similar style and are around the same size, why not buy some clothes together and set a rota for sharing them? This works especially well when you are purchasing more expensive pieces that you know you won't wear all the time.

SECOND TIME AROUND

A new invite doesn't necessarily mean you have to buy another outfit. Look at what you have already in your wardrobe and see if you can wear different pieces together to create a new look. If you are really struggling, buy only one new piece to add to the outfit, such as a top to wear with a favourite skirt or a pretty cardigan.

CHARGE IT

Many high street stores offer a 10% or 20% discount when you open an account with them and often have further discounts throughout the year. There's nothing to stop you from opening a store card for the discount then never using it ever again. If you are worried that you might put things on your card only to end up paying high interest rates, leave the card tucked away at home so you won't be tempted.

HIRE AN OUTFIT

If you've been invited to a black-tie event, hiring an outfit can be a cheaper alternative to buying one if you know you may never – or at least hardly ever – wear it again. What's more, you get the chance to wear an amazing designer frock for a night at a fraction of the price!

BORROW FROM A FRIEND

If you have a wedding or big night out coming up and don't want to buy a new dress, see if a friend has anything you can borrow instead. No one needs to know that it's not yours and you'll still feel as though you are wearing something new.

FIND YOURSELF A STUDENT

Students are often given a discount in many of the leading high-street stores. But rather than trying to pass yourself off, give your money to a student friend and ask them to buy what you want using their discount – or drag student nieces, nephews or friends along when you want to go shopping!

BIRTHDAY TREATS

Asking for vouchers from your favourite stores for birthday and Christmas presents is not only a way of avoiding unwanted gifts but it also means you can save them for when you are in need of a new pair of jeans or a coat.

DIY FASHION

GIVE CLOTHES A SECOND CHANCE

Before you throw away an article of clothing, think about whether you can use the buttons or any of the trimmings on another top to give it a new lease of life.

MACHINE MAGIC

Unless you're a whiz with a sewing machine, look for dressmaking evening classes at your local adult college to teach you the basic skills and to boost your confidence. Otherwise, ask someone who knows what they're doing to help you – it's lots of fun but mistakes can be expensive.

CUT IT OUT

When you're cutting out a pattern, always leave enough material for a little extra leeway. It's easier to get rid of excess material than to add it.

A STITCH IN TIME

Sew the garment together with loose hand stitches first and then once you've tried it on, you can easily make adjustments before sewing it with finished stitches.

BACK TO LIFE WITH A BOW

Give new life to a tired-looking little black dress by adding a wide, black silky ribbon to the waist and tying this in a big bow at the back.

LACE ACE

Adding lace to sleeveless tops or dresses gives a touch of romance and femininity while also helping to hide unforgiving upper arms.

MAKE YOUR OWN CLOTHES

Whether you want to save pennies or care about saving the environment, making your own clothes is the height of fashion. If you're a beginner, choose a dress pattern that consists of lots of straight stitching and doesn't have anything complicated like zips or pintucking. Wrap dresses and skirts are good options.

HOMEMADE MASTERPIECES

You can customize jewellery, too. Add two pendants onto one necklace, or look in a bead shop for interesting and brightly coloured beads that you can thread with dental floss to make bracelets or necklaces (floss is much stronger than thread).

CREATE BY COMPUTER

If you don't feel confident enough to customize clothes yourself, there are plenty of different companies on the Internet who will do this for you. Most will create personalized jeans and tops – and some will even do shoes.

TRAINER TASTE

Many of the big names in trainers (sneakers) offer a personalized service. You can choose your desired style, colour and even add a special message to the tongue or heel.

BIN BARGAINS

Most haberdasheries have remnant bins where they sell off cheaply pieces of material in odd shapes or the ends of lines. It's a great place to pick up fabrics you can use to customize clothes with, without having to spend money on more material than you need. If you're travelling, pick up pretty and vibrant pieces of fabric from souks or markets. You can instantly use them as belts or sarongs or create individual skirts and dresses that no one else has.

DARING DENIM

Change an old pair of jeans into a denim skirt by cutting off the legs, then cutting up the inside legs and sewing them together. Or for an even easier option, simply cut off the legs where you desire for a pair of denim shorts.

VINTAGE & SECOND-HAND CLOTHES

FIND THE REAL THING

If buying designer vintage, do your research beforehand to make sure that you are buying the real thing. Check the authenticity by looking out for metal zips and buttons rather than plastic ones. Items of clothing produced after the 1970s will have a care label sewn inside.

ONLINE CAUTION

Be wary of buying vintage on the Internet. Ask the seller questions online to check the condition and the size of the garment. Sizes have changed a lot over the years so a size 10 item from the 1950s may actually be the equivalent of an 6 nowadays. Ask the seller to measure the item with a tape measure before you buy.

KNOW THE LINGO

Brush up on vintage clothing world language. If a piece is in 'mint condition' it means the item is rare, flawless and as near to its original state as possible while 'very good condition' means wearable but with some flaws.

VANITY FAIR

Keep an eye out for vintage fairs coming to your area. They are often run by professional vintage stallholders, which means you will have an array of choices all under one roof.

CLASSIC ACCESSORIES

A great way to add a touch of vintage to a new outfit is through a bag or jewellery. Look out for statement brooches or rings in the classic style of your favourite era.

HIGH QUALITY COUNTS

Look at the fabric before you buy and where possible purchase vintage clothes made of the highest quality. Natural fabrics hang better, last longer and look more expensive. This is particularly important if you are buying clothes made after the 1960s, when synthetic materials became increasingly popular.

TIMING IS EVERYTHING

Likewise, consider your timing, too. Charity shops are always
full of clothes after Christmas and New Year and at the end of
any season.

GO FOR CLASSICS

When buying vintage or second-hand clothes go for classic
shapes and colours that you can wear from year to year.

SPLASH OUT FOR LONGEVITY

If you can afford it, it's worth splashing out on designer vintage
clothes as they do not lose their value over the years. They will
be high-quality and become a talking point at parties.

GOING IN CIRCLES

Fashion always seems to work in cycles so look for staple
second-hand items that can be reworked when the style becomes
fashionable again.

TAKE YOUR TIME

Second-hand clothes buying is all about taking time to rummage
through the rails to find a gem, so make sure you set aside plenty
of time for the job. It's unlikely that you will be able to get your
money back once you've made your purchase, so make sure you
absolutely love the items you find.

FASHION ADVICE

STYLISTS' SECRETS

SPRAY AROUND

To prevent a boob tube moving around too much or to stop ankle straps falling down on shoes, simply spritz hairspray on the inside before you go out.

ANTI-STATIC

Hairspray also works wonders by preventing static clothes from clinging to each other. Try spraying a little over your tights to stop a silky skirt or dress from sticking to them.

REMOVE STATIC WITH A HANGER

For skirts or dresses that have static cling, put the garment on, then reach up inside it with a metal hanger and brush the inside of the garment from top to bottom. For trousers, mould the hanger into a longer shape and reach up inside each trouser leg, brushing downwards.

ACQUIRE PERFECT POSTURE

Ever wondered why stars and supermodels always have such an amazing presence? It's because of their posture. Hold your head high by imagining there is a vertical bar running between each ear and shoulder and between your chin and your chest bone. To make sure your pelvis is in line, pretend an elastic band is stretched between your belly button and tailbone and try to make it shorter.

BEAT THE BLOAT

If you have a big upcoming event but are suffering from a bloated tummy, keep off the carbs and salt for 24 hours beforehand. Drink herbal teas such as dandelion and fennel (natural diuretics that make you pee more!) and eat leafy green vegetables.

BEST FOOT FORWARD

Stars look great in photos because they stand with one leg forward and their foot pointed toward the camera. Their back foot takes their body weight so they're standing almost sideways on. This creates the illusion of a slimline figure.

STRIKE A POSE

Models know how to make the best of their faces before a camera because they have had so much practice. Spend some time studying your face in a mirror to see which is your best side and whether you look better pulling a big wide smile, and at which height your chin looks best. Better still, put this into practice by pulling some poses in front of a digital camera with a friend.

STRAP-FREE, BUT SEXY

No stylist would ever dream of putting a top star in a strapless dress without a sturdy and flattering strapless bra. Not all strapless bras are created equal, however: a good one should create a great cleavage and uplift, too – not just hold your chest in place.

BE CLEVER WITH COLOUR

Stars look great because they (or their stylists!) know how to mix colours. If you're wearing black and primary colours together, accessorize and add in another colour to tone in and make the outfit look less like a uniform.

DRESS DOWN A FROCK

Get more mileage out of your eveningwear by dressing it down for the day. For example, add a cardigan and flat ballet pumps to a softly gathered 'goddess' frock for a romantic day look.

PRACTICE MAKES PERFECT

If you don't wear them often, practise walking around in high heels. Keep your weight shifted to your heel so you don't feel as if you might topple over, and take long, confident strides.

SHINE ON

For a touch of instant evening glamour, stars often apply highlighter to their shoulders and décolletage as it catches the light and gives a healthy glow and slimming sheen.

THEME IT

Stylists often work to a theme when dressing the rich and famous (cool and elegant, country chic, etc) so do the same when you get dressed in the morning. Think carefully about what you'll be doing. Will you have to walk far? Do you need layers for being inside and out? What will your surroundings be? What about a scarf to dress up or down for the evening?

SPLIT THE COST

Being a stylist is all about borrowing clothes. Do the same – but from your friends. Pinch pieces you know will suit you, or if you have seen a designer item but can't afford it, see if a friend might split the cost so you can share it between you.

STRAP IN

Paint a thin line of eyelash adhesive onto your shoulders when wearing spaghetti straps to prevent them from falling down all night.

SCAN FOR UNIQUE PIECES

Stylists want their clients to look like individuals not clones, so they pick up beautiful and interesting pieces from different countries and cultures. Do the same with a leather bag from South America or an armful of bangles from India to stand out from the crowd.

DIAMOND DAZZLE

There is truth in the saying that diamonds are a girl's best friend – which is why stars drape themselves in them at award ceremonies. If you can afford to buy the real thing, they really are a worthwhile investment and will make you look effortlessly glamorous at any special event. Good replicas are also out there, however, for a fraction of the price.

LONG-LEGGED ILLUSION

A top-secret tip from stylists for making your legs look thinner is that they put their clients in nude-coloured shoes, which makes their legs appear endlessly long. Nudes and beiges also works well with clothes in most colours.

DON'T BREAK THE LINE

When getting dressed, think about creating one continuous, unbroken line with your silhouette. Separates should be seamless, without interruptions from too-tight waistbands, creases pulling across thighs on trousers or skirts, lumps from ill-fitting bras or peeking bra straps and thongs.

FLATTEN YOUR TUM

For decades, magic or 'gripper' knickers have been a well-kept celebrity secret. All women hate their tummies sometimes, especially if an outfit is unforgiving, and these big control pants are a great solution. Just be sure to buy a pair that fits perfectly – too tight and they'll cut off your circulation, too loose and they won't do their job.

AVOIDING FASHION FAUX PAS

MID-CALF BOOTS

Unless you are very tall, mid-calf boots tend to 'cut' legs in half, making them look short and a little stumpy.

ALL MIXED-UP

Don't make the mistake of trying to satisfy everything that is currently in fashion with one outfit. You will only look as if you're trying too hard. Stick to one style at a time.

CREASED-UP MESS

What's the point in spending hours choosing the perfect outfit only to wear it crumpled? No clothes look good wrinkled, no matter how expensive they are, so always keep a good steam iron handy. If you really hate ironing, buy clothes that are made from fabrics which don't crease as much

HIGH-HEEL BOOTS

Stick to flat boots if you have to walk any distance and don't wear ones with killer heels to daytime events or you'll spend the whole day tottering around with aching feet.

VPLS

A great outfit can be ruined by visible underwear, so invest in some well-fitting, streamlined smalls. If pants still show, your trousers or skirt are probably too tight!

WATCH OUT WITH WHITE TROUSERS

White trousers can look terrible unless you are slim, so only wear them during the height of summer and if they are loose-fitting and made from a good-quality fabric that is not see-through.

DISASTER SOS

LADDERED TIGHTS

Always carry clear nail polish in your handbag – paint it on to stop surprise runs in their tracks. To prevent future ladders, make sure your tights are big enough – too small and they are more likely to rip.

EMERGENCY HEEL REPAIR

If a high heel snaps in two, coat one piece with a superglue (such as 'shoe goo') at the site of the break and try to reattach the other section. Stay off your feet as much as possible until you can change into another pair of shoes.

MEND A HEEL PROFESSIONALLY

Stop at a heel bar and see if there is anything that can be done to rescue your shoe – mending is best left to a pro. Failing that, visit your nearest shoe store and buy a pair. Ideally, keep fabric ballet pumps in your handbag for such emergencies.

RED WINE ON WHITE COTTON

Ask the barman or party host for soda water – it's the best thing for gently sponging off a red wine stain. Better still, play it safe and stick to black at parties where you know the alcohol is free-flowing!

MAKE PILES DISAPPEAR

If you're in a hurry, run a cool iron over the worst of the bobbled areas – this will flatten them – or draw a strip of Velcro along the piled fabric to remove the bobbles. Then, when you have time, invest in a pile shaver or pile razor (available from haberdashery departments) and shave your sweaters!

SHINE YOUR SHOES

Off to an important interview but you've scuffed your shoes? Smear a small amount of petroleum jelly over the toes and heels. It'll work until you can give them a proper polish.

CHEWING-GUM STAIN

Remove as much of the gum as possible with a knife and then hold an ice cube to the stain until it hardens. You should then be able to scrape off the excess. Finally sponge the area with hot water.

RESCUE STUBBORN ZIPS

If a zipper simply won't budge, try running a lead pencil along the teeth. If that doesn't work, rub a bar of soap or a wax candle onto the problem area. With a little manipulation, it should come unstuck.

RUB AWAY RAIN MARKS

Use a nail file or rough pencil eraser to gently rub away rain marks from suede, being careful not to damage the delicate surface. This should ease out the stains. Also invest in a suede protector spray and apply a layer over your shoes or jacket every couple of weeks.

VARNISH IT

Always carry a bottle of the nail polish colour in the shade you are wearing, especially if it's a dark one. You can repair small chips on toes and fingers, and while this is not as good as a re-varnish, it looks a million times better than having the chip showing.

BUTTON UP TIGHT

A loose button can quickly turn into a missing one, so dot the top with a little clear nail polish to prevent threads loosening further and the button completely falling off. Sew it back on as soon as you get the chance.

CARE & CLEANING OF CLOTHES

STIFF AND STARCHY
It might sound like a tip from the 1950s but using starch spray on cottons and linens helps keep their shape and prevents them from creasing as much. And it'll give your collars and cuffs a nice crisp finish, too.

INSIDE OUT
Turn jeans and denim jackets inside out to help prevent fading when you're washing. This goes for dark cords and bright-coloured cotton trousers, too.

EMPTY YOUR POCKETS
The first rule of machine washing is to make sure you empty all the pockets on clothes – there's nothing worse than unloading a dark wash only to discover everything is covered in white bits from the tissue you left in your jeans pocket!

HANG AROUND
Clothes that can't be tumble-dried should be placed on hangers to dry naturally. Do this immediately after they come out of the machine to reduce ironing time.

GOOD HOUSEKEEPING
To avoid last-minute panics in the morning, set aside one hour a week to iron, organize dry-cleaning and sew on buttons or tidy up hems, and so on.

COLD RINSE

A common mistake when hand-washing clothes is to use hot or warm water, but even this may damage delicate fabrics. Always use cold water and don't ever leave items to soak or they may shrink.

FLAT AND DRY

Wool loses its shape if hung out to dry. The best thing to do is to roll items in a towel to absorb excess water and then lay them out flat to dry, keeping them away from sources of direct heat such as radiators.

CLEAN DELIVERY

Check out your local dry-cleaning delivery service. Most residential areas and many larger offices have them. They make life easier by picking up and dropping off items at a time convenient to you.

BIT OF FLUFF

Remember, any clothes that shed – such as towels and fleeces – should be washed separately to avoid covering everything else with fluff

MAKING HIGH FASHION WEARABLE

DON'T BE A DEDICATED FOLLOWER

Remember that fashion trends work in opposites – low-rise trousers give way to high waists; skinny jeans hail the advent of the palazzo's return. So to be truly ahead of your time, start wearing a style's opposite partner just as the look hits the mainstream. People will think you are very stylish and a trendsetter rather than follower.

V IS FOR VERSATILITY

Study the main silhouettes of the season and spend a bit more money on a piece of clothing in one of those shapes that you can take from day to night – just add a pair of heels and some smart accessories.

PLAY IT SAFE

If you want to make just one high-fashion investment, go for a great coat or jacket – it will be the first thing people see, so pick one to suit your shape and colouring that you can rely on year after year.

LOOK FOR SPIN-OFFS

An increasing number of designers are extending their ranges to provide a cheaper version of their high-end fashion. Alternatively, look for collaborations between high-fashion designers and high-street stores to get a designer piece for a fraction of the cost.

CATWALK TO HIGH STREET

If you like a designer piece but don't want to pay the high prices, the good news is that you don't have to go without – or even wait. The average time from catwalk to high street is now as little as two to three weeks, so you can pick up a designer-inspired number that looks almost as good for a fraction of the price.

BUILD UP SLOWLY

Pay attention to what the latest trend for the upcoming season will be – such as frills or tartan prints – and buy one or two key pieces that fit into your own style. You can always add to this as the season continues if you find you're wearing the look a lot.

LOOK FOR DESIGNER DAY DRESSES

A one-piece day dress looks effortlessly chic and the bonus of buying designer is that the cut and fabric will be amazing so you'll look and feel great. Choose shirt-dresses in cotton or wrap dresses in heavy jersey – both are easily dressed up or down and won't date.

PICK WISELY

Just because designers are sending a certain look down the catwalk, this doesn't mean it will suit everyone. If you are unsure about a style, you could end up looking uncomfortable and not get your money's worth out of the item – so be sure it flatters your shape and isn't just on-trend.

THINK CLASSIC CHIC

If you're splashing out on a designer piece, choose something that will last longer than one season. A classic little black dress can be worn again and again while that fluorescent print may be pushed to the back of the wardrobe after a couple of wears.

START SMALL

Work your accessories to the max. A designer-inspired scarf or necklace can provide an effortless way of showing you've got the real thing without paying out too much cash.

AGELESS STYLE

SAY IT WITH COLOUR

While black is a fail-safe colour that can look very sophisticated as you get older, be wary of wearing it from head to toe. Team it with softer, darker colours such as deep purple or burgundy and avoid wearing too much black near your face as it can make you look sallow and draw attention to under-eye bags.

BANISH THE BAGGY

Don't think that just because you're not 21 anymore, your clothes should become baggier. Garments that are well tailored and fitted will always be more flattering and make you look instantly fashionable.

COVER TELL-TALE SIGNS

The upper arms and the neck are prone to revealing your age, so if you hate these areas on you, cover them up with scarves, shawls and sleeves.

SEX APPEAL

Looking glamorous doesn't mean having lots of bare skin on display. Show off your sensuality through fabrics such as silk, cashmere and leather in rich and sumptuous colours.

UPDATE YOUR JEANS

Keep an eye on which styles of jeans are in each season and get rid of jeans in old-fashioned shapes. Darker denim bootcut jeans will be more flattering, and while you don't want to expose yourself in very low-rise jeans, be careful with very high-waisted ones, which can give you what's known as a flat 'mum bum'.

KEEP IT SIMPLE

Go for classic cuts and shapes rather than overly fussy and frilly clothes. Look for the classic staples such as trench coats and A-line dresses for sophisticated but on-trend chic.

DRESS YOUR SHAPE, NOT YOUR AGE

When it comes to buying clothes, choose fashions that suit and flatter you rather than what you think is appropriate for your age. Don't hit a big 'O' birthday and suddenly start wearing pearls and a twinset with camel trousers! If you've got the figure, wearing classics with a fashionable twist always works.

BEWARE SCOOP AND ROUND NECKS

These are the least flattering necklines as they repeat the line of a drooping cleavage and highlight any crêpey skin. Instead, stick to v-necks, which draw the eye upwards for a more youthful effect.

TRENDY SPECS

Wearing glasses doesn't have to make you look older. Work out what shape suits your face and then look at the latest trend is for that style. Study magazines to see what celebrities are wearing and if you can, treat yourself to a designer pair.

ETHICAL FASHION

30 IS THE NEW 40

By washing your clothes at 30°C (86°F) instead of 40°C (104°F) you'll save 40% of the usual electricity consumed, making this a greener option – plus your clothes will last longer.

THINK ABOUT FABRIC

Where possible, avoid clothes made with nylon and polyester. Not only are they non-biodegradable, making them difficult to dispose of, but both are made from petrochemicals that pollute the environment and add to the problem of global warming.

GO GREEN

Look for products made from organic cotton. This is grown without the use of chemical pesticides and insecticides and so saves money for the farmer while also saving the planet. Organic wool produced using sustainable farming practices and without toxic sheep dips is also increasingly sold in shops.

FAIRTRADE FASHION

It's not just coffee and chocolate that can be Fairtrade. Look for the Fairtrade mark on cotton clothing. This ensures that the cotton is made to Fairtrade standards, which means the farmers were paid fairly and had safe working conditions.

TA-TA TO TUMBLE DRYERS

The sun and wind do just as good a job of drying your clothes as any tumble dryer. Drying them outdoors – or inside on a rail if it's raining – saves energy and also makes your clothes smell far better than using a machine. Plus it avoids shrinkage and wear and tear.

CHARITY CHIC

Green, cheap and ethical, charity shops are often the ideal place to pick up a bargain. By buying (and taking) your clothes to charity stores, not only are you helping the environment but you are also giving to those in need.

HIGH-STREET ETHICS

Many of the big high-street chains are waking up to the demand for eco-friendly products and have launched their own organic ranges. Many now stock clothes made from organic cotton for only a fraction more than the price of their ordinary ranges.

GREEN PEACE OF MIND

Everybody likes a bargain but at what cost? Sometimes there are reasons why clothes are so cheap and often it's because they have been shipped over from China or India where costs of labour are a tiny amount of the price paid. Check out the policies of your favourite stores – sometimes it's worth paying a little more for peace of mind.

TRY A WET CLEANER

Conventional dry-cleaning often uses a toxic chemical that has been linked to cancer. In the US, some states including California have already started to phase out this chemical and replace it with healthier options. The best alternative is 'wet-cleaning', which costs the same but uses biodegradable soap instead of harsh chemicals. Ask your local dry-cleaner if they offer this service.

MAKE DO AND MEND

Put your grandmother's words into practice and do some simple alterations and repairs. The rise in cheap clothing has led to some people simply throwing away clothes that could easily be made as good as new with a little cutting and sewing. It's estimated that 500,000 tonnes of unwanted clothes end up on landfill sites every year. If you're not handy with the needle, find a tailor you trust and you'll be helping out local business at the same time.

INDEX